Real World Survival

Preparing for and Surviving Disasters

Also by Richard G. Lowe Jr.

Non-Fiction

Safe Computing is Like Safe Sex: You have to Practice it to Avoid Infection
Prejudice and other Irrationalities: Human Rights and Happiness
How to Self Publish: Getting your Book out There (2015)
Sins of the Internet: Electronic Plagues (2015)
Etiquette in the Electronics Age: Turn off the Damn Cell Phone (2015)
I Я A Manager: Managing from the Trenches (2015)
Safe Social Networking (2015)
Cloak and Dagger: Controlling your Online Persona (2015)
Conquered Fears (2016)
How to Promote Your Book: Gaining Eyeballs (2016)
Dying: A Love Story (2016)

Fiction

Fur Baby: Adventures with Humans (2015)
Ghost Healer (2016)
Unanticipated Consequences: Paradox in Time (2016)
Conspiracy: Unleash Hell (2016)
Hells Bells: Hiking Through Hell (2016)
Eight Jewels (2018)

Peacekeeper Series
Peacekeeper (2016)
Battle of Bernard's Star (2016)
Treason of the Admirals (2017)
Neutron Star (2017)
Black Hole War (2018)
Invasion Earth (2018)
Earth's Revenge (2019)
FTL (2019)
First Contact (2020)
The End of Empire (2020)

Richard G. Lowe, Jr.

Real World Survival
Preparing for and Surviving Disasters
www.realworldsurvival.com

Part of the Disaster Preparation and Survival series

Published by The Writing King
www.thewritingking.com

Richard G Lowe Jr, 340 South Lemon Avenue #5029N, Walnut, CA 91789
http://www.realworldsurvival.com/ and http://www.thewritingking.com/
rich@thewritingking.com

Although every precaution has been taken to verify the accuracy of the information contained herein, the author and publisher assume no responsibility for any errors or omissions. No liability is assumed for damages that may result from the use of information contained within.

Printed in the United States of America

Publisher's Cataloging-in-Publication data
Lowe Jr, Richard, 1960-
Real world survival: preparing for and surviving disasters
/written by Richard G Lowe Jr
p.cm.
Includes index.

Library of Congress Control Number: 2015910362
ISBN: 978-1-943517-03-9 (Paperback)
ISBN: 978-1-943517-04-6 (Kindle eBook Format)
1. Survival. 2. Survival manual. 3. Disasters Planning/ I. Title.

This book is dedicated to L. Ron Hubbard, the best friend of mankind.

Acknowledgments

Many people throughout my life influenced me to write this book. As with everything, without the help, kindness, and understanding of others I would not be in the position I am today.

The Los Angeles Fire Department has earned my special thanks due to the fine CERT classes they teach on a regular basis. CERT stands for Community Emergency Response Team. I took the series of seven 3-hour classes twice, and they gave me a good grounding in the essentials of how to prepare for and survive a disaster.

I also thank my good friend Eli Gonzalez, the president of The Ghost Publishing, for his belief in me as I moved into a new career of professional writing. His knowledge of the art and science of the power of the written word is inspirational and motivated me to put on the cloak and hat of a true professional writer. http://theghostpublishing.com

My sister Belinda and her husband Ken Schmahl deserve my special thanks. They operate and own a charter school, The Schmahl Science Center in San Jose California, and I learned much from their example of the value of hard work and dedication. They helped many students over the decades and stand not only as a shining example to me but to their entire community. http://www.newprod.schmahlscience.org/

Ken Cureton has been my friend and colleague for years, through the good times and the bad. He has remained one of my closest friends for all these years. This man has strongly influenced my life with his sense of humor, honor, and integrity, and his incredible intelligence that he has put to good use.

Finally, thank you to Susan Jekarl, for reviewing this manuscript. Susan works tirelessly to inform people in California about earthquakes. For information about earthquake preparedness, check out her site www.totallyunprepared.com

The cover art for this book was designed and created by Crownzgraphics at crownzgraphics@gmail.com

Preface

Be ready for disaster. That was my motto while I worked for Trader Joe's. My team designed and built a duplicate computer room intended to run the company in the event the machines in the corporate office were damaged or destroyed. We had a huge responsibility, and we took it very seriously.

During this time, we were struck with a couple of medium-sized earthquakes, as well as a fire that came close to the office. I found it interesting that few of my team members seemed to have any understanding of how to respond to these situations. As I thought over their actions, I realized that computers are worthless without employees to run them. A major flaw in our disaster plan was people were needed to run computers, and no plans had been made to ensure they were safe and able to work. Additionally, those that we needed to operate the business had little understanding of how to prepare for and survive a disaster or emergency.

In response, I decided to take a class called CERT-LA, which is a 7-day course sponsored by the Los Angeles Fire Department, to learn more about survival. CERT stands for Community Emergency Response Team, and the purpose is to train people to be more effective during an emergency.

This class was one of the most fantastic educational experiences of my life. It was packed with information from the first day to the last, with a high degree of interaction, lectures, and practice sessions to put the knowledge to use. I took it twice to squeeze every last bit of data out of it that I could.

I was so excited when I finished. Since the class was (and still is) free, I decided I'd let everyone know. The knowledge and understanding of what to do in a disaster are potentially lifesaving, so I figured everyone would want to check it out.

I asked a few of my friends and co-workers a few questions about what they would do in a disaster. One answer from one of my teammates was typical.

"If there was an earthquake right now, what would you do?" I asked him.

"Get under the window," he answered without hesitation.

That shocked me. The right answer, of course, is to get under a heavy table or desk. Protect your body from falling objects. Getting under a window would be among the worst things you could possibly do since the glass would shatter over the top of you.

What would you do to protect yourself during an earthquake, hurricane, or other large-scale emergency in your area? Do you have a go-bag ready in case you need to evacuate? Do you keep a few days to a few weeks of food, water, and other supplies in your home?

Does all of that sound foreign to you?

I decided to write this book to pass along some of the knowledge I've learned over the years about disasters.

My qualifications

What makes me qualified to write a book about this subject?

In addition to completing the CERT-LA course twice, I was in charge of disaster recovery for Trader Joe's for 20 years. Part of that job entailed having a detailed understanding of emergencies, including how to prepare for them, how to respond, and how to recover later.

I have taken courses on the subject of disaster preparation and survival at several disaster recovery conferences, read dozens of books, and practiced the techniques as part of numerous drills.

Most of all, I want you to understand that the best way to improve your chances to survive during any emergency is to have the knowledge and to be properly prepared in advance.

I hope you never have to use this data to live through a disaster. However, if the world falls apart around you, whether from an earthquake, hurricane, or similar emergency, I trust the information contained within will have proven to be of value to the survival of you, your family, and your friends.

Introduction – when disaster strikes

Have you ever been in an earthquake or hurricane? Have you witnessed the horror of a raging forest fire or a house burning down? Have you felt the panic when you realized you were lost in the wilderness? Have you experienced a medical emergency in an area where no help was available?

I've seen my share of disasters during my life. Some were unpredictable acts of nature; others were caused by ignorance or stupidity, or by not thinking through a situation.

I've lived life to the fullest and sometimes gotten myself into situations that, although they began innocently enough, became disasters in their own right. On other occasions, the wrath of nature caught me unprepared and without the supplies and tools needed to survive.

Let me begin this book with a few examples of some of the disasters and emergencies I have experienced. It was these events that motivated me to become trained in surviving disasters and handling emergencies. I decided that the next time disaster strikes I would be prepared.

On Christmas in 1986, my father decided we were going to take a hike. The day was beautiful, warm, but not comfortable. The snow was still on the ground from the storm of a week before. Our goal was to get back before lunch, so we left early, about 7 a.m., and anticipated returning home by noon.

Our front yard bordered on the south side of the San Bernardino Mountains. Just past Route 18, there was a steep drop of several thousand feet. A small canyon wound its way down the side of the mountain. It looked very scenic, and we thought we'd easily make the trek to the bottom and back in a few hours.

We began the hike with little more than a few granola bars, sturdy shoes, and the clothes on our backs. We slipped out of the house early, simply telling the rest of the family that we'd be hiking, without informing them exactly where we would be.

Talk about the perfect storm.

Looking from Route 18 in Lake Arrowhead, from the author's personal collection

The hike down the mountain was beautiful. The small canyon soon became a stream; then it transformed into a small river filled with cold water from the melting snow. Because of the tremendous beauty of the surroundings, we soon lost track of time. We kept hiking further down the mountain, not releasing how far we had gone, and not thinking much about the return trip.

Before we knew it noon had come and gone. We climbed down a 200-foot shale cliff to discover a magnificent hidden waterfall, with a deep pool shaded by the cliffs and trees all around it. It was one of the most beautiful places I've ever visited.

We remained at the waterfall for a while, then continued further down the riverbed. As we hiked, we finally realized it was much later than we thought.

We looked back, and it finally sunk in that we had to climb back up that mountain to get home.

Our common sense kicked in and we began the long hike back up the mountain. My father suddenly grabbed his chest and exclaimed that he believed he was having a heart attack. He sat down, looked at me, and told me to hike out of the canyon and get help. To make matters even worse, it started to snow.

These were the days long before cell phones existed, and even if they did it is doubtful that we would have gotten cell service way down in that canyon. I looked at my father, turned around, and began struggling to get back to where we started.

To make a long story short, I finally climbed out of that canyon at 8 p.m. At the end, I was guided by the voice of my mother and sister as they walked around the top of the canyon calling our names. Breathless, I explained to them and a fireman named Kurt about the hike and my father's condition. Kurt took off down the mountain, and eventually found my father covered in a pile of leaves to keep warm.

As it turned out, my father was fine. He didn't have a heart attack after all; it was probably just the stress of the situation. The firemen airlifted him out with a helicopter the next day and named the place where he was found "Lowe's Meadow."

My father and I could have avoided this emergency with some simple preparations. We didn't bring any food, water, or supplies. We vastly underestimated the distance involved, didn't tell people where we were going and hadn't even looked at the weather report.

The lessons I learned from this emergency were to research and prepare. In future hikes, and there have been many hundreds of them, I always performed basic research. I checked the weather, let someone know where I was going and my estimated time of return, and I carried some emergency supplies, food, and water.

A few years later I commuted every weekday from our house in Lake Arrowhead to college in San Bernardino, which is a very scenic and pretty drive on a long and twisty road. I loved that drive, with the beautiful scenery, trees, streams, and animals. It was very relaxing.

One hot summer day as I was driving down the mountain I realized the sides of the road were on fire. The trees and shrubs were burning all around me. I looked back and saw the fire had jumped the road; I couldn't go that way. Everywhere I looked there was fire. Honestly, at that moment I thought I was going to die.

I saw a fireman running towards me, radio in hand. I stopped and let him into the passenger seat. He told me to drive slowly forward and then talked on his radio. A few minutes later, as we were getting close to the fire in front of us, he told me to stop. I had no idea what he was doing; there was fire in all directions.

Suddenly the car was immersed in water. Afterward, I learned the fireman had directed me to drive to an open spot on the road, and a helicopter dumped water directly on us. After that, I was able to continue my trip down the mountain.

Unfortunately, the fire, which was one of the larger ones in California history, ruined the scenic drive. Instead of beautiful trees, green shrubs, and forest animals, there was blackened earth and burned logs all around.

I had been completely unprepared for a disaster of that magnitude. I had no idea what to do or where to go. In fact, if I had been paying more attention, I might have avoided being trapped by the fire in the first place. The lesson I learned was to pay attention to my surroundings.

A few years later, after my wife passed away from lung disease, I became fanatical about getting out into nature. For two years, I visited a different scenic spot in the American Southwest each and every weekend. I put more than 100,000 miles on my car traveling from place to place to try to keep my sanity after the loss of my wife, who was also my best friend.

One weekend I decided to go on a long hike in Joshua Tree National Park. I believed I was prepared; I wore a vest with pockets full of supplies, carried enough water for the day, had more than enough food, let the rangers know where I was and had examined the maps of the area thoroughly. I carefully checked the weather and was happy to learn it was going to be a clear and sunny day. I did notice there was a prediction for some rainstorms in the local mountains, but I didn't think much about it because those areas were over 40 miles away.

I was about four miles into the hike when I heard some strange sounds, kind of a gentle roaring in the distance. The weather was perfect, with barely a cloud in the sky, and the only thing I could see were a couple of other hikers in the distance.

Something, perhaps some sixth sense, alerted me that I'd better get to higher ground. I had been hiking in an old, dry riverbed because it was easier due to the lack of rocks, plants, and trees. I decided to move quickly to the rocks nearby. These were sheltered by a few trees, so it seemed like a good place for lunch.

The volume of the roaring increased, and I looked around and noticed a massive wall of water crashing down the riverbed where I had just been hiking. I watched in fascination as the water swept by, washing away bushes, shrubs, rocks, and anything else in its path.

If I had not left the riverbed when I did, I would certainly have been swept away by the water and drowned. Even though I was perfectly safe on my perch on the rocks, I was terrified. I had no idea what had happened, but I was determined to find out.

A few hours later I ran into a Ranger, and he told me what I had seen is called a flash flood. Rainstorms or snow melts high in the mountains can cause them. Sometimes storms that are 50 miles away can create walls of water flooding all of the dry creek beds in the area. He explained there had been a series of rainstorms in the mountains bordering Joshua Tree National Park, which caused the flash flooding.

If I had stopped at the ranger's office before heading out on my hike, they would have been happy to brief me on the local conditions, including the possibility of flash flooding. That was the lesson I learned-acquire an understanding of the local conditions and phenomenon from the experts.

But that's not the only disaster I experienced. Early one morning I was awakened by a low rumbling sound and a gentle shaking. My eyes snapped open, and I bolted straight up in the bed. A few seconds later the whole room swayed from side-to-side for what seemed like an eternity. I pushed my wife out of bed onto the floor and watched as the furniture came alive and started dancing all over the apartment.

I was amazed at how much everything moved. The kitchen table slid six feet like a demon possessed it; the bookshelves rocked back and forth as if they were drunk. The coffee table somehow found itself in another room. Books became missiles; CDs flew off the shelves, threatening to kill or maim anyone in their path. The refrigerator moved across the floor to the other side of the room, spilling its contents everywhere. Glasses and plates tumbled out of the shelves in the kitchen, shattering all across the floor, sending sharp shards of glass everywhere.

It seemed as if the Mad Hatter had taken control of our apartment, rescinding the laws of physics for those few moments of time. Some invisible insane person tossed our belongings all over, willy-nilly, without a care as to whom or what was damaged.

That shaking was one of the most terrifying 30 seconds of my life. Luckily, neither my wife nor I were hurt nor was there damage to the apartment. Besides a few broken dishes and some shattered CDs, nothing was destroyed.

However, our son was missing. My wife, Claudia, jumped up after the earth stopped moving, screaming his name. She ran, barefoot, into his room, and then emerged seconds later in a complete panic. He was not in his bed; he was not in the bedroom. In fact, he was not in the apartment at all. My wife screamed for her son, yelled that I needed to do something, looked under things, and ran (again barefoot) outside, still screaming.

At that moment, Claudia started crying because her feet were bloody. She had run, barefoot, over the broken glass in the kitchen. We didn't even have a first aid kit. I had to use towels and scotch tape to bind up her feet and stop the bleeding.

We found our son the next day, after a full 24 hours of stress and insanity. He had decided, as he often did, to put on his headphones and walk around the neighborhood. He was a couple of miles from home, in downtown Hollywood, when the earthquake struck, and found himself in the midst of a terrified crowd of people in complete blackness. The power went out immediately, and he was stranded, miles from home, with no way to contact us, no food, no water, and only a few dollars in his pocket.

These days when I think back to those terrifying seconds more than 20 years ago I shudder at how unready we were for a disaster. We were regular people leading normal lives. We believed we didn't need to prepare for emergencies. We didn't even think about it before that day.

As these events proved, we were unready, and we hadn't taken the time to become aware of our surroundings. We didn't educate ourselves, plan and rehearse for emergencies, or stock up on supplies. We had not properly prepared our environment and ourselves for anything that might happen.

Because we were unaware of the environment, we had no idea how to get help, or even if help was available. We didn't know the location of the fire department, and because the phones stopped working, we didn't have any way to communicate with anyone outside of our immediate area. We had no understanding of the city's emergency plans, and no idea of what help if any, they could provide.

We didn't have a stock of supplies; we didn't even have a first aid kit, not even one of those almost useless $10 kits from the drug store. We didn't have a flashlight, extra batteries, bottled water, or extra food.

It's a wonder we survived at all.

If you follow the steps in this book and understand the concepts, you will be better prepared for any disaster, from a simple car accident all the way to a major earthquake or a hurricane.

Disasters can strike anywhere at any time, with or without warning. Sometimes they can just affect you, as with a car accident, or they can affect an entire nation, as with the terrorist attack on Sept. 11. Taking a few simple steps to gain knowledge and squirreling away some supplies can mean the difference between living through a disaster and not surviving at all.

The key is to be ready and to know what to do when one occurs. There is a balance, as with anything, and it's important to find that middle ground of preparedness. It's vital to be prepared, but it's equally important not to wrap your whole life around the possibility of disaster. Those who are not prepared find themselves at a loss, even to the point of injury or death, when an emergency occurs. Those who are overly prepared lose out on the normal, non-disastrous parts of their lives (presumably the majority of their time on this earth).

In other words, building a bomb shelter 100 feet underground in the remote Rocky Mountains stocked with five years of survival gear and food is *not* the best way to spend your money and live your life. On the other hand, it is prudent to know at least the evacuation routes, so you are prepared if your city needs to be evacuated due to a hurricane.

A good place to start is to sit down one night and ask yourself what kind of disasters are likely to happen in your area.

- Are you living in earthquake country (California, for example)?
- Is your town located in a likely path for hurricanes (New Orleans, for instance)?
- Does your area suffer from tornadoes?
- Do you live near a freeway? In a high crime area?
- Is there a chemical plant nearby? A nuclear power plant?

You will also need to know your responsibilities in a disaster (at least your prediction of them).

- Yourself
- Your family
- Pets
- Neighbors
- Random strangers who come to you for help

Answers to these questions will help you determine what you need to consider when educating yourself on possible disasters, as well as direct your purchases for your survival kits. Don't be alarmed; a survival kit is as simple or as complex as you want to make it. A simple duffle bag containing a dozen items might be all you need.

Table of Contents

Who can you depend on?

Who can you depend on after a calamity? Surely the government will send help to a disaster area immediately, right? Don't the authorities have teams and organizations in place, ready to send help to any area that needs it?

Katrina

Hurricane from space (Public domain photo, courtesy pixabay.com)

In last August 2005, a monster hurricane, one of the largest in United States history, struck the Gulf Coast. Katrina, a Category Five, killed more than 1,800 people. Additionally, thousands were missing. A large portion of New Orleans is below sea level, so when the levees collapsed much of the city was flooded.

Government agencies at all levels, local, state and federal, were overwhelmed by the magnitude of the disaster. The delayed and incompetent response by federal agencies such as FEMA needlessly increased the human suffering and costs of this tragedy.

Many people sat on rooftops for days in the harsh sun, pounded by rain and the elements, while the water swirled around them. They had no food or water, no shelter, and no help.

I was amazed as I read about the disaster, safe in my home in California. The Gulf gets hit by hurricanes every year, and yet the majority of the people living there were totally unprepared.

Even more astounding was the amount of time it took for people in the area to receive help. It was weeks before any significant aid arrived, and it took months to set up temporary housing and start to sort out the mess.

A friend and I drove through New Orleans in 2013, on our way to Florida, and even then, more than eight years after the hurricane, the devastation was still obvious. There are whole areas of the city which are fenced off because they are uninhabitable, and people continue to live in temporary shelters.

When will help arrive?

Normally you can depend upon the authorities for help in the event of a local disaster such as a house fire, building collapse, or flood. Fire, police, and similar departments constantly prepare and rehearse for these types of events and have the manpower and procedures in place to deal with them.

Of course, it will take time for that help to arrive, which is dependent on where you live, the weather, the condition of the roads, and any other emergencies that are occurring at the same time. How quickly help is dispatched also depends upon the nature of your emergency.

As the scope of the disaster increases, the chances of help arriving decrease dramatically. After a large earthquake or hurricane, for example, you may not receive assistance for days or even weeks. Disasters of this scale require intervention from state or federal levels, and that requires time to coordinate and get into position.

You should prepare to be without help for a minimum of three days. In a large disaster, such as a significant earthquake or hurricane, plan on being more or less on your own for two weeks.

In the event you need to evacuate, your go-bag(discussed at length later in this book) needs to contain food and supplies for a couple of days. This gives you time to get to the evacuation shelters. MREs (Meals Ready to Eat) are perfect for this purpose. You can order them by the case; just toss the boxes into the trunk if you have to leave in a hurry. Your supplies should include several 5-gallon full, sealed water bottles, you can throw those into the trunk of your car as well.

What about utilities?

Do you know what you would do without any services? How would you fare if the electricity stopped working for days or even weeks? What would you do if the toilets cease to work, there was no trash collection, or water no longer flowed from the taps?

Depending upon the nature of the disaster, you may find yourself without any utilities or other services. The best thing you can do is to plan for any contingency by stocking up on food and water, creating a go-bag or two, and ensuring the rest of your disaster plan is complete and implemented.

Electricity

A complex network of towers, cables, and substations delivers power to your home. All of this is vulnerable to many types of disasters. Earthquakes and floods can destroy towers, fires can burn cables, and explosions and accidents can destroy substations.

The electrical grid in the United States is, for the most part, adaptive. If one component fails, the system can reroute electricity around the failure. For example, if a fire destroyed the lines going through a forest, power will be routed through other wires that are still working.

Still, in a disaster the power can fail and remain inoperable for days or weeks at a time. Make sure your disaster planning includes contingencies for power failure.

Actions you can take to prepare include:

- Stock up on batteries for flashlights and radios.
- Purchase one or more Universal Power Supplies (essentially large rechargeable batteries) and keep them plugged into the wall. With a UPS, you can charge cell phones, laptops, tablets, and so forth.
- Buy a portable generator.
- Install solar power panels.

Gas

Some homes are fully electric while others use gas for cooking, fireplaces, and heating water. Natural gas is normally odorless; the gas company adds the rotten egg smell so the gas can be detected if there is a leak.

During a major disaster such as an earthquake, one of the first things you should do is turn off your gas at the main. Some homes and apartments are equipped with special switches in their mains to automatically cut the gas if the earth shakes more than a certain amount.

Some of the actions you can take to prepare for the loss of gas are:

- Purchase one or two of those small propane camping stoves.
- Ensure you have warm clothing and blankets.
- Purchase camping blankets for your go-bag.

Water

Water travels a long distance from the reservoir or tank to your home. In some cases, there are hundreds of miles of pipes, tanks, canals, dams, and various other storage methods and channels. A disaster can damage these systems.

For example, in Southern California the aqueducts and canals that deliver water to the area run through many fault lines. In a major earthquake is it likely that these will be severed, which will stop the flow of water.

Other disasters can cause damage to pipes so that the water still flows but is polluted with bacteria, sewage, or chemicals. In this case water will be delivered to your home, but will be unusable.

Repairing water lines could require days, weeks, or even months. In your disaster plan, you need to decide how much water you want to store for drinking, and how to provide water for washing and bathing.

Actions for you to prepare for water shortages include:

- Store enough water for two weeks for you and anyone living with you. You need at least one gallon (3.78 liters) or water per day per person. The five-gallon bottles delivered to your home by the local water company will last one person for five days.
- Purchase a dozen collapsible water jugs.
- Purchase water decontamination kits from your local camping outlet and store them in your go-bag.

Sewage

As with water, the sewer system is a complex series of underground pipes, tunnels, and treatment plants. In a major disaster, the sewage system will often cease to function. This means water will back up into your home if you flush the toilet, take a shower, or wash your hands in the sink.

Because sewer and water pipes often are side-by-side in the ground or cross each other now and then, your drinking water can be contaminated. Thus, it is a bad idea to drink any water directly from your faucets after any emergency.

You must include the possibility of the sewage system not functioning in your disaster plans.

Purchase several boxes of large trash bags. During a disaster line your toilet with these to capture waste products. Use one bag to line the toilet; insert that bag into a second bag and seal it with twist ties for safe keeping until trash service is restored.

Trash collection

Out of all of the utilities, trash collection is among the most vulnerable because it depends completely on people. During major disasters, roads can be blocked, and fuel for the trucks can be in short supply, preventing trash collection. The people who drive the trucks may be injured or chose to remain at home due to the emergency.

Thus, trash may remain uncollected for long periods of time: days, weeks, or, in extreme emergencies, months. Large amounts of uncollected trash can produce diseases and attract insects and animals.

When you consider how to survive a disaster, you need to include plans for how to store and dispose of your trash.

Some things you can do in advance include:

- Find locations, such as an area of your backyard, to store trash until it can be collected.

- Purchase several large boxes of trash bags with ties to use for trash.

Cell phones

Have you even thought about what you would do if your cell phone service stopped working for a day or even a week at a time? How would you communicate?

You cannot count on your cell phone being operational during a disaster. The calamity, whether it is a hurricane, earthquake or storm, could damage the system itself. Even if the system survives, so many people make calls during disasters that the cell system itself will be swamped and rendered inoperable.

Also, the police may intentionally turn off the cell phone system because of a terrorist attack or police action. This is done to prevent communications by malicious individuals, and to prevent remote detonation via phone call.

What can you do to prepare?

- Use your Internet connection for email and phone calls.
- Install a landline if you can.
- Ensure your phone is fully charged each day.
- Purchase an Uninterruptable Power Supply and keep it plugged in at all times. The battery will provide a power source to recharge your cell phone, laptops, and tablets when the power is out.

During the disaster, try texting as that may continue to work even if the phone service is overloaded.

Internet or cable services

Your home phone or cable service is another complex system that in most cases supports television, Internet, and phone service. You cannot rely on this service remaining active after an emergency. The service itself could cease operating, or the power could go out, which effectively prevents you from using it.

There is not a lot you can do to prepare in advance for the failure of Internet or cable services. You can purchase a hand-cranked or battery-powered radio to receive the news during a disaster, or come up with other alternatives for receiving information.

If you are extremely concerned about access to the Internet during a disaster, you can contract with a satellite phone provider. Note that these services are extremely expensive, and their service level is not great.

Situational awareness

Improving your odds of surviving is a simple matter of becoming aware of your environment and raising your consciousness. You need to remain aware of your surroundings and what is happening around you whenever you can.

Simple? Well, not really. Most of us spend our days half asleep, wandering from place to place without looking around. Quite often, we don't even know where we are, much less who or what is behind us, to each side, and even in front of our very eyes.

Even ignoring the effects of drugs, smoking, and alcohol for the purposes of this discussion, people move from day to day without sensing (seeing, feeling, smelling, touching) anything at all. People often just exist. They go from place to place and only see specific things; they miss so much, and that makes them vulnerable, and ill prepared for what can, and often does, happen.

I first became aware of situational awareness simply because I made a right turn and almost hit someone who had stepped off the curb just as I was turning. I was looking to the left to find the opening in the traffic so I could dart out into the lane, and I didn't see the poor lady. Worse, she didn't see that I was getting ready to make that right turn and didn't notice that I was not looking out for her movements. Thankfully, I did spot her out of the corner of my eye, slammed on the brakes, and missed hitting her by less than an inch. One split second of hesitation, one exceptionally small moment in time, and both of our lives would be different today.

Although that little incident is not in the same scope as a major earthquake or a hurricane, for the two of us it would have been a disaster. To make it worse, it would have been an entirely preventable disaster. Had each of us simply been awake and paying attention to our surroundings it wouldn't have happened. To state it in even simpler terms, being fully aware of our surroundings would have eliminated the possibly of disaster.

Look around you. Just look. Don't draw any conclusions. Don't get upset, and don't make any decisions. Just look around. Believe it or not, this is the first, and perhaps the most important step of being prepared for any disaster- knowing where you are and what is around you.

Wherever you are reading this book raise your eyes and look at your surroundings. Look at the floor, at the walls, at the doors, the ceiling, the furniture, and anything else in your environment. If there are people, notice the direction they are traveling, where they are coming from, and where they are going.

As you look, you should begin to notice patterns. In an airport, you'll see people moving to the terminals, getting ready to get on their flights. In a hospital bed, you see the room and its contents, and you'll note the location of the windows, doors, and perhaps another person sharing the room. In your house, you'll see walls, the floor, and the ceiling, as well as furniture.

Let's say you are in a theater, getting ready to watch a movie. You've sat down in the chair, and you're reading this book on your tablet, killing some time until the movie begins. Raise your eyes upwards and look around. Note the screen in front of you, the projection booth behind you, and the location of the exits.

How far are you from the doors leading outside? How many people are between you and those exits? Where are the steps? Are they to each side of the rows of chairs? Where are you in relation to them? Are there people on each side of you? In front of you? Behind you?

You might notice additional details such as how many children are around you and where are they located? Is the theater relatively clean or is there trash and other debris in the area?

Taking the time to look takes all of one or two extra minutes at the most. You don't need to spend a lot of time looking. You are not drawing any conclusions; you are not allowing yourself to feel any emotions. You are simply noting the location of people and things, and where you are in relation to them.

Now, with just this one simple step, you are vastly better prepared for any emergency or disaster than you were just moments ago.

Why?

Let's suppose you finished looking around, then settled back to watch your movie. Towards the middle of the movie, you smell smoke, a lot of it, but there is no alarm. The smoke smell gets worse, and people are starting to look around. If you hadn't taken a moment to locate yourself in the environment, you would have to spend that time now, in the heat of a disaster, figuring out where to go, what to do, whether to stay or run. But since you've looked, and since you know where you are, you can immediately, without panic, do what you need to do to survive.

When you sat down and looked, you saw there were crowds of people in front of you, but fewer behind you. You saw that in addition to the exits to the front, there is an emergency exit behind you to the right, not as obvious, but there nonetheless. Instead of panicking and running towards the front through crowds of terrified people doing the same thing, you have the option of moving back to the exit behind you, where there are fewer people in the way.

Let's say you are at school, taking a class in geology. When you entered the room today, you sat down, then located yourself in relation to the environment. You noted the location of the doors, the windows, the desks, the closet, and the people. If there was an emergency, say a gunman is shooting randomly, you would have increased your chances of survival, simply because you know where you are. You could go through the door into the hall, jump out the window (or not because you know you are on the third story), hide in the closet, or crouch under a desk.

Now carry this a little further: as you travel from place to place. On occasion just look around and note what's happening around you. In other words, keep your eyes open. Don't forget about your other senses as well. Listen, smell, touch; these are all tools that you can use to your advantage.

Now you are better prepared for whatever happens.

Types of disasters

The news media makes it seem like there is a disaster of some kind or another every day. They are always reporting on a calamity that struck somewhere in the world. At times, it can seem completely overwhelming. In fact just a few days ago I read that a volcano erupted in Japan, killing several dozen hikers; just a few weeks ago a major fire was threatening a small town with destruction. Everyone had to be evacuated, but fortunately, the fire was controlled before any damage was done.

Street being flooded (Public Domain, courtesy pixabay.com)

In general, however, most of us live the majority of our lives without facing a life-threatening disaster. When I lived in California, I was in constant fear of "the big one" (the major earthquake that was supposed to happen at any time). However, in the 52 years I lived in that state only three moderately sized earthquakes occurred. These were frightening and caused some inconvenience for my family and myself, but our lives were not in danger.

A big part of preparing for disaster is understanding what is likely to happen in your area.

Chemical spills

Out of all disasters, this is potentially the worst and most damaging. A major chemical spill can occur without warning from industrial plants, nearby transportation routes, or from underground pipes. Large-scale spills require immediate evacuation and depending on the magnitude of the problem, you may never be allowed to return.

Chemical storage tank (Public Domain, courtesy pixabay.com)

Earthquakes

The night was cool, and the street was empty except for an occasional homeless person. Al enjoyed wandering the Boulevard in Hollywood; the lights, shops, and crowds helped him relax and unwind. Deep in his thoughts, the 17-year-old lost track of time. His tranquility turned to terror at 4:30 a.m. when the ground started shaking. Al watched in horror as the light poles swayed back and forth, the walls of the buildings leaned outward, and the cars nearby bounced on their wheels. He had no idea what to do or where to go, and when the lights of the city went out, he sat down, curled up into a ball, and cried.

Have you ever been in an earthquake? I've been in a couple of relatively large ones and I can say they were terrifying. The feeling of helplessness is profound. While the earth is shaking there is no time to think or do anything except perhaps to throw your body under a table. Yes, get *under* something; the triangle of life you've read about on the Internet will most likely get you killed.

I was amazed at how much everything moves. Heavy tables, huge computers, cars, huge blocks of concrete, and everything else can move astounding distances in just the few seconds or minutes that the earth is shaking. Objects fly out of shelves and off walls, to shatter on the floor or smash into any people in the area.

If you live in an earthquake zone, you need to prepare in advance. Once it happens, there is nothing you can do, and, if the quake is large enough, the whole area around you will be smashed beyond belief. It may be days, weeks, or even months before basic services such as electricity, sewage, or gas are restored. You may not even be able to go to the store for food.

Optimum survival requires a well-stocked pantry with enough food, water, and toiletries for at least two weeks for all family members and a few friends.

Damage to home after earthquake (Public Domain, courtesy pixabay.com)

Fires – local

A friend of mine had a small fire in her house. It started as just a trash fire, but before long the wall started to burn. In a panic, she threw a blanket over the fire and put it out. The cost came to thousands of dollars, and she had to spend a week in a hotel while her place was repaired.

She was lucky as it could have been much worse. Fortunately, only property was damaged, and no one was hurt. What can you do to prepare for a small disaster such as this? Look through your renter's or homeowner's insurance to make sure your coverage is adequate and includes sufficient living expenses for a few weeks to a month in a hotel.

© Dalesemt | Dreamstime.com - House On Fire Photo

Fires – large scale

In 2007, there was a huge fire in the Lake Arrowhead Mountains that burned over half a million acres, destroyed 3,069 homes and other buildings, and killed 17 people. More than one million people were displaced, in one of the most devastating fires in the history of California.

How do you prepare for a fire of this magnitude? Is it even possible to have a plan to cope and to handle the consequences afterward? In this type of emergency, your preparation must center on the ability to evacuate quickly. You need a well-provisioned go-bag, a solid communications and evacuation plan, and a good understanding of the local area.

Floods

Katrina bore down on New Orleans. Victoria and her family were terrified. They had no idea what to do or where to go, so they remained in their home, trusting everything would be fine. As the hurricane hit they huddled together in one corner of the house, afraid of every noise. Their worst fears came true when the water rushed into their house, and they had to run hurriedly up the stairs to avoid drowning. They spent the new few hours on the roof waiting for rescue.

Water can suddenly burst through dikes and levees, dams can break, and rainstorms can cause dry rivers to fill faster than a person can run. These events, whether local or statewide, can be devastating. If you are in a flood zone of any kind, you need to prepare and practice evacuation plans, have your go-bags ready, and understand your options if flooding occurs.

Flooded streets (Public domain, courtesy pixabay.com)

Hurricanes

Next to earthquakes, hurricanes are probably the most terrifying and devastating disasters of all. Katrina swept right over the top of my sister-in-law's home, and she spent two weeks on the road moving from place to place until she could return. We went frantic in California trying to figure out not only where she was, but even if she was alive.

As with an earthquake, several states could be devastated. Utilities such as electricity, sewage, trash collection, gas, and phones could be unavailable for weeks or even months.

How can you possibly prepare for that magnitude of disaster? You need a good emergency plan, a well-stocked pantry, a good understanding of the local and state evacuation routes, one or more go-bags, and excellent insurance coverage.

Nuclear disasters

The nightmare scenario is a nuclear disaster of one sort or another. If you live near a nuclear power plant, you will want to have good evacuation plans, go-bags, and iodine capsules or tablets for all family members.

Nuclear power plants (Public domain, courtesy pixabay.com)

Power outages

I experienced a three-day long power outage while I lived in California. It happened during the hottest part of the summer and was a miserable experience. In this case you will not need to evacuate; a well-stocked pantry is helpful since the food in your freezer and refrigerator will be spoiled.

Rioting and looting

A single event such as a strike at a manufacturing plant, a well-publicized police shooting, or an unpopular trial verdict can trigger civil disturbances. In the case of a riot, stay home, lock your doors and windows, and wait for instructions from the authorities.

Tornados

These funnels in the sky cause tremendous damage. Wind speeds can exceed 250 miles per hour, and the storm can cover one or more square miles. Your options during a tornado warning are to take shelter in a tornado safe room if possible, or get to the lowest floor of a building and make yourself secure. Beforehand, you need to find tornado shelters, create a communications plan, and make sure you have adequate insurance coverage.

Tornado (Public domain, courtesy pixabay.com)

Tsunami

A huge wall of water can follow any earthquake that occurs in the sea or ocean. Depending upon the circumstances of the tsunami, there may or may not be notice and time to evacuate. Tsunamis cause immense damage and, as with hurricanes, recovery can take years.

Disaster information

Receiving an early warning of certain kinds of disasters can give you and your family an opportunity to prepare and to make some decisions about what to do. Of course, disasters often come with no warning. Earthquakes, for example, do not announce their arrival in advance.

You can subscribe to services that will keep you informed about recent events and, in the case of weather, for example, will send you advance notices.

Pacific Disaster Center

Website: http://www.pdc.org/

If you live in the area around the Pacific Ocean, then you should download and install the Disaster Alert app on your iPhone or Android device. This handy app will keep you informed about any disasters and severe events in the Pacific area. The app is free, although there is a small charge if you want to receive just local alerts.

Their website contains valuable information about any current emergencies taking place.

National Weather Service

Website: http://www.weather.gov

The U.S. government operates the National Weather Service, which tracks all weather in the country. They maintain a website that is an excellent source of information about weather and weather-related events.

All of the information on the site is free and is a source for every other weather service in the United States. Rather than using any of the other weather services, I've found it best just to go straight to weather.gov for weather information.

US Geological Survey

Website: http://earthquake.usgs.gov/earthquakes/

Notification service: https://sslearthquake.usgs.gov/ens/

If you are in an earthquake zone, you should become familiar with the U.S. Geological Survey website. This site gives up-to-the-minute information about earthquakes all over the world without the emotional biases of the news media.

Sign up for the notification service to receive emails or text messages about earthquakes in your local area.

Community Emergency Response Team (CERT)

The best training you can get for emergencies is provided free by many local fire departments. These courses span seven or more evenings and go over everything from preparing for disaster to an actual disaster simulation.

The purpose of these programs is to help you, your family, your neighbors, and your neighborhood in an emergency situation.

You can use a search engine to find the next class or call your local fire department.

These classes will prepare you for the disasters that are likely to happen in your area. You will also learn about fire safety, search and rescue, and so on. The idea is to enable people in the community to assist others before help arrives from professional responders such as the police, fire department, and medical services.

Severe weather warnings

Numerous services will warn you about weather and other problems in your area. Although these cannot warn you of every possible disaster, they can inform you of bad weather in your area, fires, and other events that can be predicted or are in progress. After an incident, such as an earthquake, occurs these services can provide additional information about dangers and evacuation orders.

Creating the plan

Do you and your family know the location of your gas meter? How about the police station? Are you aware of any dangers in your area such as underground gas mains, chemical plants, and hazardous materials storage? Do you know how to get quickly out of your residence if there is a fire?

Getting the answers to these and other questions, and using those answers to create a plan, will improve your chances of surviving.

Do you share your home or apartment with roommates or family members? If so, a good way to start your disaster planning is to sit down with them and discuss how to prepare and respond to emergencies. You'll want to cover these topics:

- Frankly discuss probable emergencies
- Discuss the various locations where each individual might be when a disaster strikes.
- Get everyone involved in the planning and implementation of the emergency procedures. Even children need to be involved because they have special needs and a unique point of view that can be useful.
- Specify two locations to meet, one outside the house in case of a fire or other event local to your home, and the other outside your neighborhood if it is impossible to return home.

Tools such as Google Maps® may be used to research the locations of businesses and organizations that might be useful in a disaster. It is important to print this information because you may not have electricity or Internet access after a disaster happens.

Keep a journal of your findings. Anything you print should be inserted into your binder. Organize it with tabs for different kinds of information.

Store this journal in your go-bag, so it is in a known location and at your fingertips if needed. Keep the notebook updated as circumstances change. It is best to review all of the information at least once or twice a year to ensure it remains up-to-date.

Research your area

Google Maps® is a great tool to begin the research into your local area. Go to http://maps.google.com and enter your street address. The map will locate your address and center it on the screen. You can use the zoom function (the + and – symbols in the lower right of the screen) to zoom in and out from the map.

Use the Search Nearby link located in the box on the upper left to find the location of various types of businesses and government offices. You'll want to find these locations:

- Hospitals
- Police stations
- Fire stations
- Grocery stores
- Hardware stores
- Gas stations

Press **Ctrl-P** to print the screens and save them in your disaster planning notebook. You can use the back function on your browser to move back once you've printed each map.

You can also use Google Maps for the directions between your residence and various other locations, such as the police station. Print out each of these and store them in your disaster planning notebook. These locations include:

- Your children's schools
- Each of the homes of your friends

To give you an example of the power of this technique, look for nearby police stations. To do this, click the *Search nearby* link under *Explore this area.*

Your cursor should move back to the search box. Enter *police stations* and click the *hourglass* button to list the police stations in your area, along with a map. Use **Ctrl-P** to print this screen.

In the box on the upper left, you will see a list of police stations that are in your area. Click on one of them to get more information. Part of that information is the website address of that organization or business. Click on that link to go to the official website.

Map sure you print out the homepage for each of the following:

- The fire station
- The police station
- The nearest hospital

Put these into your disaster notebook.

Scout the area where you live
Once you have all of your maps printed and bound in your disaster planning notebook, take a few drives around town. Bring your notebook with you, and visit each of those places. Make any appropriate notes on the back of each map.

By doing this, you get familiar with the routes to each place, understand any obstacles, and identify any hazards. You might note, for example, that the route to the police station goes over a bridge that could collapse in an earthquake, or the road may be hazardless during a storm. This type of information will be useful should a disaster occur.

Locate any dangers
Are there dangers to your safety in the area around you? A chemical plant? Superfund sites? Buried natural gas lines? Are they any kind of manufacturing facilities?

Take a drive through the streets of your immediate neighborhood and look around. Make note of any high tension wires, potentially unsafe bridges, manufacturing facilities, and so forth.

One extreme danger that is not quite so obvious is any transportation routes such as a railway, freeway, or expressway. Any route upon which freight can travel can pose a risk of spills, derailments, and accidents.

Underground gas lines, oil pipelines, and large electrical transmission lines can pose a significant risk in a disaster. For example, in an earthquake, the shearing effect of the earth moving can rupture national gas lines, creating the possibility of large scale explosions.

A major portion of New Orleans is below sea level. The city is kept dry by seawalls, called levees, which keep the water from getting into the city. Your research and travels around town should uncover these kinds of constructions.

With this information at hand, you can make decisions about how to prepare for possible disasters. In the case of New Orleans, for example, you might decide to purchase flood insurance, or to store your survival supplies in the upper stories of your home.

Evacuation plans

Sabrina never imagined that she would need to flee her town and spend a few days in a school recreation hall because of a fire. Yet here she was, three days after being told to evacuate, still not knowing when or even if she could return home. The minutes after the police knocked on her door were spent frantically gathering up a few things, running to the car, and driving thirty miles to the hall. She just wanted to go home, assuming the fire had not destroyed it.

Some disasters require evacuation from the area. The authorities may decide during times of emergencies such as hurricanes, floods, riots, and so forth that it is best for the populace to leave the area.

Research your home

Create a floor plan of your home and make a few copies. You can use these to note exits, the location of specific items, such as your medicines, and for general comments. As you go through the following sections, make notes on those floorplans.

Exits

The fire started in the kitchen. The shrill screech of smoke alarm woke up Helen abruptly. At first she sleepily thought it was another false alarm, but the smell of smoke soon jolted her fully awake. She quickly jumped out of bed, and upon touching the door handle, realized she couldn't get out that way. Knowing she might only have seconds left, Helen looked around frantically, saw the window, and ran towards it. She had to push a desk out of the way and because it was painted shut, break the glass. She got out, but it was close. The fire destroyed her house, but she survived.

Locate all of the exits in your residence. Evaluate each one to determine if, in an emergency, it could be used to get out quickly.

Take out one of your floor plans and ensure that you mark at least two escape routes from each room. Make sure everyone in the household can use those exits. Sometimes these escape routes can be especially challenging for disabled or chronically ill people, so think through how everyone can get out during your planning phase.

Physically stand in each room and examine each exit. Can any lock be unlocked from the inside without a key? Does the window or door open, or has it been painted or otherwise sealed shut? Is the way to the exit clear or will furniture or other objects need to be moved for access?

Handle any issues with using each exit. Keep in mind that if the exit cannot be used, it is not an exit. You don't want to find that out during a fire or other disaster.

Electrical panel

Find the electrical panel for your home or apartment. Each home has a panel or two mounted on a wall in an out-of-the-way place such as a closet, the laundry room, the kitchen, or even in a bedroom. Usually, there is just one panel, but in a large residence there could be more. A metal door with a latch typically covers the panel.

Make sure this is not locked, and if it is, ensure the key is available. It's a good idea to hang a flashlight near the panel to use if the power goes out.

Gas meter

If there are any gas appliances in your home or apartment, locate the meter. These are generally in the rear of the building, although they can be anywhere near the building. Each meter (and there may be more than one in a multi-unit complex) is a metal canister with a pipe on each side and a dial in front.

Examine the main to locate the shutoff value. It will be on a pipe to one side. Make sure you own a wrench that fits the bolt on the shutoff valve. Keep the wrench in a handy place. In the event of a disaster, you might need to shut off the gas. You'll use the wrench to turn the valve. Don't practice this procedure, because if you shut the valve off you will need to call the gas company to turn it back on.

© James Boudreaux | Dreamstime.com

Emergency contacts

Create an emergency contact list. You can use any number of products to store and track this information, or just keep it in a spreadsheet. You can even do it this old fashioned way and write everything down in your notebook.

What do you need to record in contact list?

- Friends
- Family members (Include some family and friends that are far from your area)
- Police Department
- Fire Department

- Local hospitals
- City Hall
- Local grocery and hardware stores

Keep printouts of your emergency contact list in your disaster planning notebook. Be sure to update it as needed with new or changed contacts.

Special needs of children

Children have special needs during disasters. They are easily frightened and can be very emotional.

Create a go-bag for your children and include books, games, and toys that do not require electricity.

If you have smaller children, you should include diapers and other supplies in their go-bags. As your kids grow older make the appropriate changes in their supplies.

People with disabilities and chronic illnesses

Leo had lung disease, and he needed an oxygen machine to survive. The machine had a battery that lasted about two hours. During a long power failure, he had a real scare because he thought the battery would run out before the power was restored. Fortunately, the electricity came on, and he was fine, but it was a close call.

Include anyone with a disability in your planning for disasters. People with disabilities often have special needs, such as medications, health machines, caregivers, and service animals.

Each person with a disability needs to complete a personal assessment. Start by making a list of personal needs and plans for providing for those needs in the event of an emergency.

Some of the questions you need to consider during this preparation include:

- What plans should you make to care for any service animals after a disaster?
- If you need assistance with showering or personal care, how will this be provided for after a disaster?
- Do you require any special tools, utensils, or equipment for your basic survival needs?
- Do you require equipment, such as an oxygen machine, which requires electricity?
- Do you need a wheelchair to get around? How will you deal with the possibility of debris blocking your path?
- Do you require any special medications? Do you have enough on hand most of the time for several days?
- How will you get out of the building or area in the event of an emergency? If the elevators are not working, how will you get down the stairs?

Answer these and other questions so that in the event of a disaster you are better able to survive.

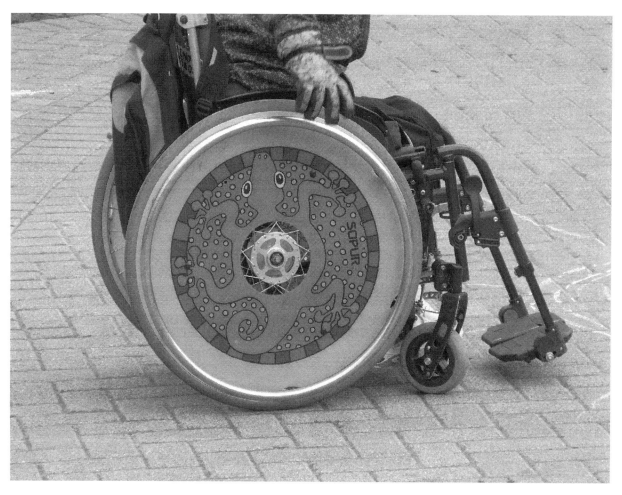

Wheelchair (Public domain, courtesy pixabay.com)

If you have an electric wheelchair or scooter, you may want to keep a manual wheelchair to use in case the electricity goes out for long periods of time.

Carefully examine exits, ramps, stairways, and elevators and think through your options if they are blocked or inoperable. Also, consider how you will get to shelter. For example, typical tornado shelters are in the basement. If you are disabled, how will you get down the stairs?

Pets

During the massive, half-million acre fire in Lake Arrowhead in 2007, some of my friends were required to evacuate. They hurriedly shoved a bird in a cage, a small dog, and their cat into their station wagon and headed for the desert. Needless to say, it was a hair-raising journey, made even worse because they had to find food and water for the pets.

Have you made plans for your pets during a disaster? How will you feed, water, and provide for their other needs? What will do you with them if you are required to evacuate the area?

Ensure there is enough food and water in your plan to last them for a couple of weeks at least. You can also create a go-bag just for your pets with food and other supplies you might need.

Communications plan

Communication (Public Domain, courtesy pixabay.com)

It is important to create and rehearse a disaster communications plan.

Find someone you know out of town who will be the contact in the event of a disaster. Make it clear to everyone that they are to call this contact person instead of fanatically trying to call each other during an emergency. Identify several people who can serve as emergency contacts in case someone is unavailable.

During any major disaster, the phone system may be disabled. Even if it is technically working, it is likely that so many people are trying to call in or out that it is unusable.

A little-known fact is the long distance part of the phone system is often separate from the local phone system. Thus, the local system may be overloaded and unusable, but you can still make a long distance call.

Of course, the Internet may still work even if cell phones or landlines are not functional.

Texting may work even if the voice portion of your cell phone service doesn't or is overloaded.

Below is a sample family and friend communications plan. Use this plan for a major emergency affecting more than just your home.

If the emergency is local to you or your general area, get yourself to safety if possible and call 911.

If the emergency is for a larger area, an earthquake, for example, then follow the procedures below.

1. Barbara in New York is the primary contact. Sally in California is the secondary contact.
2. If the Internet is still operational. If so, email Barbara and Sally with details of what happened and the status of family and friends.
3. Send a text to both Barbara and Sally. State the nature of the disaster (earthquake, tornado, or whatever it is) and the status of family and friends.
4. Wait a few minutes. If you receive an acknowledgment from either Barbara or Sally, do not attempt to call them.
5. If Sally or Barbara do not acknowledge, attempt to call them and, if you reach them or their voicemail, give a brief status.
6. Do not call locally unless necessary.
7. Every hour, for as long as communications are operational, send an email and a text to Barbara and Sally with your current status.
8. If you want to know the status of anyone, communicate with Barbara or Sally.

All family members and friends who want to know what is happening should, according to the plan, call the primary or secondary contact. No one should attempt to call into the disaster area; in fact, it is very likely communications into the area will not function.

If any family member is within the disaster area but not at home, they should contact the primary and secondary emergency contact.

By using this method, you will ensure there are two people outside the disaster area who, assuming any communication at all is functioning, have up-to-date status information.

Rehearse the plan at least twice a year. Your test could be as simple as sending an email and a text message to the primary and secondary contacts telling them you are testing and asking them to reply.

Preparing your home

Have you looked around your home with the thought of possible disasters in mind? A few minutes performing an inspection can save your life or prevent severe injuries later.

Some of the actions you should do include:

- Look for windows that might shatter. Consider alternatives to secure them, including coating them in window film (for earthquake regions) or replacing with hurricane glass.
- Find cabinets that can fly open. Install cabinet latches to keep them closed.
- Inspect all wiring in your home for breaks and frays. Do not hide extension cords under carpets, as they can suffer hidden damage.
- Locate any shelves or other items that can fall and block the exits from rooms or the residence. Move those to different locations.
- In earthquake areas, use earthquake hooks to anchor pictures and frames to the walls.
- Locate any heavy items that are high up on top of shelves or appliances. Relocate these items to lower areas.
- Consider using two-sided tape or museum putty to hold items to shelves. You can also install a guardrail on shelving to keep things from falling out.
- Many homes are not bolted to their foundations. During an earthquake, hurricane, or other disaster, the home can shift from the foundation and be heavily damaged. Get your house inspected and if it is not bolted down, make the appropriate correction.
- Inspect your roof and chimney for loose objects, such as bricks, that can fall. Repair them.
- If your home is in a fire zone, ensure you clear the area around it as required by local regulations. It is best to clear all brush at least 100 feet from your home.

Fire extinguishers

I was cooking dinner one night and got distracted by a phone call. I smelled smoke, turned around, and saw there was a fire in the pan. I grabbed he fire extinguisher, pulled out the pin, and tried to put it out. Much to my surprise, instead of putting out the blaze, the fire was just blown all over the kitchen. Fortunately, I had some boxes of baking soda and managed to put it all out before any damage occurred.

The moral of this story: learn how to use your fire extinguisher before you need it.

Fires can spread very quickly, and a readily available fire extinguisher can mean the difference between minor damage and complete destruction. Install a fire extinguisher near the kitchen and the garage, and at least one per floor of your home. Put them in plain sight, not in a cabinet, so they can be used without delay if needed.

Always place a fire extinguisher in the kitchen, because fires start there most often. Many fires start because of hot grease. Be sure the extinguisher is not placed near the stove, because during a fire you will risk burns. Place the fire extinguisher on the wall near the kitchen.

Make sure you install the correct type of extinguisher, and that you know how to use it. Also, be sure you perform maintenance at the recommended intervals.

The best option is to complete your local CERT class. Fire extinguisher use, care, and safety is part of that course.

Secure shelves and appliances

In an earthquake or hurricane zone, it is a good idea to secure furniture and appliances to the wall where possible. Bookcases, refrigerators, and display cases can topple and fall over. Secure them where possible, and be aware of their location so you know areas to avoid when looking for shelter.

Strap the water heater

If your home is in an earthquake, tornado, or hurricane zone, you must ensure your water heater is strapped to prevent it from rupturing. If the tank falls over, hot water and natural gas may leak and cause damage, injury, and even explosions.

Water heaters are also good sources of clean water after a disaster. A typical tank holds between 30 and 50 gallons of water, all of which can be used after a disaster if the tank remains intact.

Kits are available which include all of the hardware needed for strapping your water heater to a wall.

You need to use heavy gauge metal strapping (not duct tape) and secure the tank from the center and top. There should be no more than two inches of space between the water heater tank and the wall. If there is more space than this, attach a block to the wall with lag screws.

Smoke detectors

Ensure your home has smoke detectors on each floor, especially near bedrooms. Test these at least once per year. If any smoke detector does not work, get it fixed or replaced without delay.

Stocking up

The best way to stock up for an emergency is to include your disaster supplies as part of your normal routine. For example, purchase canned food and store it in your pantry or other location, and eat out of that supply.

Be sure to rotate your stock. To do this, put new stock in the back and pull from the front when you use the product. This will prevent your food and other items from expiring.

The idea is to keep at least two weeks (more if you can) of food, water, and other necessary supplies in your stock. In the event of a major disaster, it is likely that help will not arrive quickly. Two weeks is a good number to plan around.

Begin your stockpile by ensuring you have a can opener or two on hand. Keep at least one in a place where it is easily found, but will not be used or lost during non-emergencies. Can openers, as a rule, tend to wander all over the place because they are needed all the time.

Trash bags

Imagine there's been an earthquake, although not the "big one" everyone's been terrified of for decades. Just a medium sized, scare-the-hell-out-of-you shaker. You survive without injury, and everyone in the area is doing fine. Sure, the power is out, and there is no gas, but you have some supplies, and it's only a matter of time until the utility companies come around and fix things up.

But now you notice there is no water coming out of the tap. Fortunately, you have a dozen five-gallon bottles of water in the garage. You think you have it all covered.

That is, of course until you notice that the toilet doesn't flush. You think it's not a big deal until the power is out for a few days, and the bathroom stinks to high heaven because the waste has nowhere to go. Insects are crawling all over the place, and your home is becoming more and unlivable, even though there was no damage at all.

Here's where a little secret mentioned by the fireman at the CERT group would come in handy. The speaker, a 20-year veteran fireman, suggested you keep a few boxes of trash bags among your supplies. Simple, ordinary trash bags.

What this allows you to do is line the toilet with a bag. You "use the facilities," then close the bag with a twist tie and put that inside another trash bag. Now you can safely store your waste practically anywhere for as long as needed. You can pile the bags in a big trash can or bin, or simply stack the bags in the backyard. When the disaster is over and done, and trash service is resumed, the bags just get hauled away.

Water

In 1994, there was a break in the water main down the road. At the time, the Metro rail was being constructed, and somehow the excavators pierced the large pipe that brought water to our house. We were without water for about the whole day. My wife was panicked because we had no backup supply of any kind, except a couple of six-packs of diet soda. I went to the local grocery store to see if I could find some water, only to find out everyone else apparently had the same idea. There was none for sale. I had to drive about ten miles before I found a store with water.

The example above was just a minor inconvenience. Now imagine an earthquake, hurricane, or other disaster occurring in your area. Would you have enough water on hand for you, your family, your pets, and possibly neighbors and friends for a day? A week? A month?

There are things you can do to get water if times are desperate. Some of the tips given in the CERT (Community Emergency Response Team) include:

- If you have not treated the water in your toilet tank (don't worry about the bowl) with chemicals (tables or bottles of cleaner) you can use it.

- The water in your hot water tank.
- Other sources of water such as melted ice cubes (if not contaminated), bottled water, juice from canned vegetables and fruits, and so on.

You may also be able to find water in external sources such as streams, ponds, and wells. Just be careful not to drink any that might be contaminated, especially with chemicals such as oil.

Without water, your survival is at risk. Planning ahead is simple, and the cost is minimal.

- Store one gallon of water per day per person and pet.
- Keep a bare minimum of a three-day supply of water for every person and pet in the household.
- If you have the space, keep a two-week supply.
- Rotate your water, using the oldest first. Drink this water in your normal routine so it does not go to waste.
- Keep an eye on the expiration dates.
- Ensure your go-bag has a bottle or two of water purification tablets.
- Keep a bottle of unscented liquid chlorine bleach, which can be used to disinfect your water. Make sure the bleach is pure and does not contain perfumes or soap.

A great way to keep a supply of water on hand is to subscribe to one of those home delivery water services and order a few extra bottles. You can store those large, five-gallon bottles for six months to a year. One caution: do not store the bottles on cement or concrete. Chemicals such as lye can contaminate plastic water bottles left on cement (like in a garage). Store your bottles on a wooden pallet, not directly on the cement. Of course if your water is in a glass container you don't need to worry about anything being leeched.

I have four 5-gallon bottles of water in my home. As I receive new bottles each month, they go to the back of the storage, and water to drink is pulled from the front. This ensures that the water remains drinkable and does not become contaminated due to age.

If you suspect the water has biological contamination, then boiling is the best treatment. Of course, this assumes you have a heat source. There are tablets that you can purchase to treat water. These are very effective at killing any microbes contained in the water. It's a good idea to order a bottle or two and keep them in your go-bag for an emergency. They are very inexpensive and are useful on camping trips or hikes.

Lastly, you might want to purchase half a dozen folding one-gallon containers from any outlet that sells camping equipment. These are useful for quickly gathering water once a disaster has happened. For example, one thing you'll want to do when a disaster strikes is to open each tap in your house (sink, bathroom, etc.) and get as much water from them as possible. Usually, there will be a few gallons in the pipes even if the water has been shut off. These handy folding containers store easily and are extremely valuable if the water is shut off.

Food

I remember Katrina, even though I was living in California at the time. My sister-in-law and her family had a home in New Orleans. Their lives were severely impacted when that massive hurricane swept through Louisiana. It seems strange to me that my sister-in-law was completely unprepared for disaster even though hurricanes and storms are a normal, yearly occurrence in that area. She didn't even have a flashlight, bottled water, or more than a few days' worth of food. She was entirely dependent on the food she could scrounge from the neighbors and whatever she could get from emergency centers. She survived the disaster, but it would have been much easier with a little preparation.

It is very important to remember that even a small disaster may cause your utilities such as power, water, sewer service, trash collection, and natural gas to fail. Part of your disaster preparation must include the assumption that your home or apartment will be without power for several days or weeks, which is critical because it affects how you stockpile food.

If the power goes out and remains off for any length of time, you are going to lose all of the food inside your refrigerator and your freezer (with the possible exception of horizontal, top-opening freezers.) Remember, every time you open the door of your refrigerator and freezer you lose cold air. I've found that the food inside will last perhaps as long as a day or two as long as you don't open the door.

You should not consider the food in your refrigerator and freezer as part of your emergency stockpile. Instead, you need to store dry and canned goods; you want food that will not spoil if the power goes out and the freezer and refrigerator get warm.

I have about two weeks of canned goods in my pantry. These include canned vegetables, meats, beans and so forth. A good mixture of protein and carbohydrates is essential. People do not survive well on a diet of candy bars and frosted flakes.

All food has an expiration date, and it is important to be aware of this and incorporate it as part of your stockpiling plan. There are some things to remember:

- You should use the stockpiled food as part of your day-to-day meals. Pull any food you use from the front.
- As you purchase replacement food, add it to the back of the supply.
- Once every six months or so, it's a good idea to look over all the expiration dates of the items in your stockpile to ensure that no out-of-date items remain. Discard any food that goes out-of-date. What I like to do is pull out food that is within a month or two of the expiration date and donate it to the local food bank.

What should be in your stockpile?

- Canned vegetables
- Canned meats such as tuna, salmon, turkey and chicken

- Canned beans or similar items for protein
- Food bars high in protein, granola bars, and power bars.
- Nuts and trail mixes
- Dried fruits
- Canned soups
- Bottled water (I keep four 5 gallon water bottles at all times)
- Vitamins
- Spices and sugar, salt and pepper

Be sure you have at least one can opener. It would be very frustrating to be unable to eat the food because you can't open the can. Keep a second can opener in your go-bag.

Finally, ensure everything in your stockpile is something you will include in your normal meals, or you will find yourself throwing out a lot of food as it expires.

Canned foods

All types of canned foods are a good idea when filling your panty to prepare for a disaster. Their advantage is they have a long shelf life and do not require special storage. You can stack them on a shelf in your kitchen, pantry, or any other place in your home you can find. I would not recommend storing them in the garage or other outdoor locations, as moisture can cause the cans to rust.

The advantage of canned foods is they do not require heating. You can just eat the food straight out of the can if you'd like; you can eat canned food if the power or gas is out and you have no means to heat your food.

You will need to create a rotation system for your canned goods, so they don't expire. Stack them up on shelves, organized by product and brand. In other words, put all the canned peas in one or two rows, the corn in another, and the spinach in another. As you purchase new cans of food, place them behind the ones already on the shelves.

You will also want to inspect the dates occasionally. Once a quarter (every three months) is a good rule of thumb to ensure that the soon-to-be-expired product is removed, used, or donated. Expired food is not edible and cannot be used for survival after a disaster.

MREs

Purchasing a few cases of MREs (Meals Ready to Eat) is a good option for long-term food supply. These are totally self-contained meals, which can be eaten straight out of the bag or box. You can also heat them. They are designed to last years without refrigeration, and if you store them in a cool place, they will last over a decade.

Each MRE comes in a tough package designed for travel and outdoor conditions. Inside the bag, there is one entrée and a side dish such as rice, corn, or fruit. They also come with pepper and salt, some candy, and even sauce packets. If you prefer them hot, you can purchase them with chemical heaters for a small extra charge.

The military designed MREs to provide one-third of a person's daily calories (1,250 for each pack), vitamins, and minerals. A person should be able to survive on three MREs per day, plus of course water.

Many companies sell MREs by the case or in multiple-case lots. I purchased six cases of 12 from MRESTAR at http://www.mre-meals.net/. I highly recommend the products from this company.

If you want to learn more about MREs, a good place to start is http://www.mreinfo.com/. That site contains full descriptions of all of the different options available.

Dried food

Dried beans and similar foods are excellent to keep in storage as part of your emergency and day-to-day food supply. These products store for long periods (not as long as canned goods) and provide large amounts of protein and carbohydrates.

However, dried foods are vulnerable to moisture, insects, and rodents because they are sold in plastic or cloth bags. As with all foods, you need to have a rotation scheme in place so older foods do not expire before you can eat it.

Flashlights

Are you ready if the power is out for hours, days, or even weeks at a time? Do you have more than one or two flashlights in your home? Are they in a location you could easily get to them if the lights went out?

Flashlights are an important part of any survival plan. I recommend purchasing some rechargeable LED flashlights. These plug into a normal wall outlet where they constantly remain charged. They are not powerful, but they will help you maneuver around your home in the dark. You should verify they work properly once a year or so by turning them on and seeing how long the light lasts. Throw them out and replace them when they no longer hold a charge.

For more light, get a dozen or so larger flashlights and store them in a location that is not difficult to find in the dark. A cupboard in the kitchen or a linen closet in a hallway is an ideal spot. Do not store flashlights with batteries in them, because batteries will leak over time and render them useless.

I find battery-powered camping lanterns are ideal for emergency use. They are available online and at numerous stores that sell outdoors supplies. You can also find flashlights with a hand crank, eliminating the need for batteries altogether.

Batteries

Do you have a stock of batteries ready to power your flashlights in the event of a disaster? My plan includes enough batteries to last a couple of weeks for each of the flashlights and lanterns in my kit. To find out how long batteries last, turn on each type of flashlight and lantern you have and keep it on until they stop working. Make a note of that length of time and from there figure out how many batteries you want in your stock.

Keep in mind that batteries expire after a few years, so you will want to rotate them just like any other perishable item. Your quarterly or yearly inspection should include examining battery expiration dates, and old batteries should be thrown out.

Don't throw batteries into the trash, because they leak toxic chemicals into groundwater. I have a large jar that I fill with old batteries. When no more will fit inside, I bring it to the local recycler. Be sure to put a piece of tape over exposed terminals of 9-volt batteries to prevent shorting.

Universal Power Supplies

For many reasons, it is a good idea to purchase a few Uninterruptable Power Supplies (UPS) and keep them plugged into the wall. These are vital for computers and other electronics (such as televisions) to prevent damage due to power failures and surges.

They serve another purpose during disasters. These are large batteries and can store quite a bit of power. I keep a couple plugged into the wall in isolated areas of my home. In the event of a disaster, they can be used to charge cell phones and laptops, and to power various electronic devices for short periods of time.

Generators

If you are concerned about having power during a disaster, you might consider getting a home generator. These provide far more power than batteries or Universal Power Supplies and can also power appliances such as refrigerators and microwave ovens.

The disadvantage of generators is they require fuel that can be difficult, if not impossible, to store. For those who live in apartments, a generator is not a good option for this reason.

Another option is solar panels. If you own a home, you can install permanent panels on your roof, and portable versions are available for apartments and mobile homes.

First aid kit

Everyone needs to have one or more first aid kits in their home, their car, and their office. You can purchase a small kit from just about any store, and larger ones are available online.

I prefer building a kit from scratch because the pre-built ones just don't have the right mix of supplies for my needs.

Communications

Cell phone coverage is often one of the first forms of communication to fail in a disaster. Cells phones are dependent upon cell towers, which need electricity, and they use land lines to connect to the main communication grid. All of this is vulnerable to earthquakes, hurricanes, floods, major fires, and other large area disasters.

Landlines are a good alternative. Note that local and long distance calling are handled separately. Calls to local numbers may not work due to the volume of people calling during a disaster. You might still be able to make a long distance, out-of-state call, which is important to remember when creating your communication plan.

Medications

If anyone in your household requires any medications, prescription or otherwise, ensure you have included this in your planning. What I did for medications is purchase a watertight plastic box with a handle. The box fits on a shelf in the kitchen. My medications get stored in the box, which is small enough to fit into the go-bag. In the event of a disaster, the plan is to grab the box and put it into the go-bag.

Your gas tank

The city has been ordered to be evacuated due to an oncoming hurricane. You rush to gather a few belongings and shove them into the back of the car, grab the cat, and you, your wife and two kids jam in as best you can. You slam the car into reverse, take one last look at the home you've lived in for the last five years, then drive down the block to the freeway. As you pull into the jammed onramp, as directed by the national guardsmen, you look at your gas gauge and realize you won't be going very far. There is no way to back up or leave the freeway to fill the tank, so you get about a mile before the car runs out of gas. Since your car is blocking traffic, the police push your car off the freeway. You, the cat and the family are jammed into the back of a military transport truck.

You've lived in Los Angeles for years, always knowing the "big one" could come at any time, but because the earthquake never happened, the whole concept of being prepared slipped away. One evening in the summer, the big one hits and you and your family are lucky to have survived without as much as a scratch. You get into the car thinking you'll drive out of the city to your aunt's house in the country, and head on over to the gas station to fill up the almost-empty tank. You've acted fast, so it only takes a couple of hours to get through the line of people who had the same idea. By the time you reach the front of the line your car is on fumes. The attendant tells you "cash only" because the credit system is not working. Because you have no cash on you, the attendants push your car into the street, and you have to walk through the two miles of the devastated city to get back home.

A simple, yet important task you can perform every day as go about your business is to keep the gas tank of your car full. I make an effort to ensure that my tank never goes below three-quarters full.

Think about what has happened after a disaster. One of the first things to fail is electricity. In a hurricane, the power lines are blown down by the wind and the substations may be damaged by flying debris. During an earthquake, power plants themselves may be destroyed, power lines heavily damaged and substations obliterated. Without power, most gas stations will not be able to pump fuel at all. Those that still operate may charge exorbitant, "emergency special" rates to try to skim a little profit off the disaster.

The upshot of this is you will probably need to make do with the gas in the tank of your car at the time of the disaster. So if you make keeping your tank full every day a regular part of your life, you will have given yourself a boost towards surviving that disaster. The best news about this little hint is it does not cost extra; you have to put gas in your tank in any event so keeping it full doesn't cost any more money.

Other supplies

As you do your research and form your disaster plan, you'll determine what other supplies you may need. For example, in the past I had two pairs of tennis shoes. For my day-to-day life, I didn't need anything else. During a particularly hard rainstorm, I learned the hard way that it's a good idea always to have a good pair of waterproof work boots available.

Other supplies you need will become obvious to you as you proceed through the research, organizing, and testing stages of your disaster plans.

What's a go-bag?

"Everyone is required to evacuate immediately," the police announced over their megaphone. "The fire is headed this way. Evacuate immediately."

With those dreaded words, Sam rushed to his closet, grabbed his go-bag, and ran out the door, stopping only long enough to lock it behind himself. In just a few minutes, he was on the road and heading out of the danger area.

On the other hand, Joseph was not prepared. When the evacuation order came, he frantically ran around the house to grab a few things that he thought might be useful, throwing them into a plastic garbage bag. After leaving his home, the bag tore, and he lost most of his supplies. Not that it mattered much because the items he grabbed were not of any real value.

If you do nothing else to prepare for disasters, take the time to create a go-bag (also known as a bug-out bag.) A well-stocked g-bag is by far the most important piece of your survival plan, so spend some time and a little money and do it right.

A go-bag is a place to store your disaster survival gear and supplies. In the event you must leave or evacuate, you grab the bag and go, hence the name. Even if you don't evacuate, all of your essential survival gear is stored in that one place.

Prepare the go-bag in advance, well before any disaster. Fill it with all of the supplies, tools, equipment, and anything else you, your pets, and your family will need to survive.

Purchase a good quality duffle bag, something on wheels with a handle is ideal. That way you can cart it around without having to carry it on your back or in your arms. I prefer a duffle bag with lots of pockets with zippers on the outside. It adds a bit of extra storage and allows the supplies to be organized.

Store your go-bag in an out-of-the-way closet, under the stairs, or someplace similar. Make sure the location is dry and easy to get to when needed. The last thing you want to be doing if you have to evacuate is to shove around furniture or climb upstairs to the attic to get your supplies.

You may want to consider creating more than one go-bag if you have several pets or children.

Each go-bag needs to contain enough supplies for at least a couple of days for each person and pet. These are to handle your short-term survival needs. If you are away from your home for longer than a few days, you will need to supplement your supplies.

A good go-bag should contain the following at a minimum:

- A good can opener that includes a bottle opener.
- A change of clothes and shoes. In my go-bag, I've included two pairs of older jeans, two shirts, underwear and four pairs of socks.
- $100 in small bills; mix $1 and $5 bills, nothing larger.
- Some high-energy food such as Clif or granola bars.
- A dozen Meals Ready to Eat if possible. These last for years are lightweight, and 12 should feed one person for three days.
- One or two LED flashlights and at least one change of batteries. You might also consider one or two hand cranked flashlights.
- Waterproof matches. You can purchase these at any store that sells sporting goods.
- A couple of lightweight ponchos.
- A couple of camping blankets. These are exceptionally lightweight and small.
- A hand-cranked radio.
- A copy of each of your important documents (driver's license, insurance information, passport, contact information, and so on) in a waterproof bag.
- Along with the important documents, include a medication list (with dosages and timing) for each medication they need.

- Store extra medications for each family member. Just remember to rotate medication out of your go-bag occasionally, so it is not expired when you need it most.
- Copies of each of your keys, at the very least for your house and car.
- A good first aid kit.
- Dust masks.
- A pair of pliers, useful for many things, including turning off utilities.
- A whistle.
- A few garbage bags.
- A copy of your disaster plan with contact information, maps for evacuation routes, and a map of the area.
- A few rolls of toilet paper.
- A tube of toothpaste, brushes, and floss.
- Supplies needed for children if appropriate.
- Feminine supplies.
- Spare batteries for everything in your go-bag that needs batteries. Store these in waterproof bags or containers.
- Several bottles of water purification tablets.
- A small camera with non-rechargeable batteries (and some extra batteries).
- If you have pets, either create a separate go-bag for them or include a few cans of food for each one.

Documents

Gather together your important documents and makes copies of them. Put them all in a waterproof bag or container, and then store that in your go-bag.

The documents you need to include are:

- Your passport and visa.
- Driver's licenses.
- Birth, death, and marriage certificates.

- Bank account numbers. A copy of a canceled check for each account is perfect.
- Statements for each of your bank accounts, credits cards, money market accounts, and so on.
- Copies of your automobile, medical, life, and home insurance policies.
- Any military or other IDs you might have.
- A recent photo of each family member.
- Health, dental, and prescription cards for each family member.
- A list of medicines and allergies for each person.
- Paystub.
- If you own a gun, include a copy of your license to carry if required.

There is no telling what you will need in a disaster, so go through your important documents and decide if anything else would be useful.

Be aware of the security of these documents. Keep your go-bag secure, just as you would your wallet or purse. These papes are sensitive, personal information and it's important that it not fall into the wrong hands.

However, during a severe emergency, the most beneficial place for these documents to be is within your go-bag.

First aid kits and other medical supplies

Every go-bag needs a first aid kit. You should also keep one in the trunk of your car and another in a cabinet in your home. You can purchase first aid kits at just about any grocery or camping store. Alternately, you can purchase the items separately to make your own kit to satisfy your specific requirements.

At a minimum, the kit in your go-bag should contain the following items.

- Medical pocket guide.
- Bags for biohazards. These are used to dispose of bandages and other potentially contaminated items. You can purchase official red ones, or just include a few one-quart plastic bags.
- Face masks.
- Gauze in various sizes.
- Cotton pads in various sizes.
- Bandages in various sizes.
- Antiseptic towelettes.
- Wound closure strips.
- A couple of elastic bandage wraps.
- Aspirin or your favorite pain killer.
- Triple antibiotic ointment.
- Hydrocortisone cream.
- Digital thermometer.
- Scissors.
- Tweezers.
- Bottle of eye wash.
- Alcohol pads (you can buy these in a box of 100 for just a few dollars).
- Burn gel.

Store your first aid kits in waterproof containers and mark them clearly.

Insurances

Have you reviewed your insurance policies for disaster coverage? You should do so before disaster strikes.

Be sure you understand what types of disasters can happen in your areas.

- Are you in earthquake country? Homeowner and rental policies do not normally include earthquake coverage. You need to purchase it separately if it is available at all.
- Is your home built in an area subject to flooding? In this case, you will need to purchase flood insurance, which is a separate policy, often provided by a different insurance company.
- There may be specific exclusions for other types of disasters. Make sure you understand likely disaster scenarios in your area and balance your coverage to cover those.

Homeowners

In preparation for disaster, I went over my renter's insurance policy line by line. I spent over two hours discussing every option with my agent, raising one coverage, eliminating another, and adding a few others. I made sure I had the highest possible coverage for additional living expenses, which provide for expenses if I was unable to live in my apartment after a disaster.

Create an inventory of everything in your home. At the very least, list the higher value items. If you have receipts, copy them and keep the copies in a safe place. I scan all of my receipts into my computer and use an online backup service, Carbonite, to maintain copies elsewhere.

Your inventory should list each item, including a description, location in your home, model number, serial number, purchase price and date bought.

If you have valuables such as art or jewelry, have them appraised. Also, it is a good idea to take photos of any higher-value items.

Once you've completed this task, meet with your insurance agent to validate that you are carrying enough insurance to cover your needs. Make sure you understand whether your policy is for actual value or replacement cost. Discuss which option is best for you with your agent.

Preparing for trips and outings

One of my favorite pastimes is traveling. I love to jump in my car, point it in a direction and drive until I reach something interesting. I've probably gone on more than 1,000 road trips all over the American Southwest, and I've learned a lot about what to do, and what not to do.

Planning is important before going on any trip, regardless of whether it is just for a few hours or a several-week long outdoor adventure. Obviously the degree of preparation will vary based on the length of the adventure, the destination, and the activities planned.

For a short trip to hike at the local state park, you might only need to check the weather and glance at the park's web page. A longer day trip might necessitate reading several websites, making hotel reservations, and picking up a few supplies.

Some of the tasks you should consider doing before going on any excursion include:

- Research your destination (or destinations).
- Stop at the local ranger station or visitor center to find out the local conditions from the experts.
- Always check out the weather forecast
- Tell someone where you are going and when you expect to return.
- Ensure you have the correct supplies for the situation.

I've learned from hard experience that a few minutes of research and preparation can mean the difference between a wonderful, fun adventure and a miserable, horrible day.

Research the area

Some of Jim's friends mentioned they had a great time camping in Death Valley National Park a few years ago. He'd never been to the place, but he loved the desert and he enjoyed hiking and camping, so one day in July he hopped in the car and made the long trip.

When he arrived at the visitor center, he noticed there was a large thermometer hanging on the wall. A sign next to it proudly proclaimed, "The hottest place on Earth!" A plant blocked the view of the temperature reading.

Jim had driven in air-conditioned comfort in his car, listening to music and enjoying the ride. However, when he opened the door of the car, he discovered what "the hottest place on Earth" meant. He walked over to the thermometer and saw that it read "147 degrees."

Jim went back inside his car, closed the door, turned up the air conditioning, and drove a couple of hundred miles to a California beach. It was still hot, but at least he could get out of the car without being cooked.

Before you head out on your trip, do a little bit of research to understand the area. The Internet has a huge number of resources that can help you research just about any area on earth. If you are a member of an organization such as AAA®, you can visit or call for their advice and help.

You can use any of the Internet-based mapping applications. For example, Google® and Bing® both have excellent versions that are completely free. Take advantage of these to map out your route and possible alternatives before you go.

National, state, and local parks are all described on official and unofficial websites. You can find information about virtually any destination in the world on the Internet. Use this vast wealth of data to educate yourself before your visit. Not only will you be better prepared, but you will most likely find out about other things to do and experience because of your research.

Talk to the experts

During the spring of 2004, I decided to take a trip to a beautiful state park called Anza-Borrego in Southern California. I stopped at the visitor center, pulled the camera out of my trunk and started snapping pictures of the nearby plants, insects, and scenery. I saw some beautiful shrubs, about twice my height, covered in what appeared to be yellow puff balls. As I got closer, I noticed some gorgeous insects, about two inches long, flying all around the tree. I moved very close to them, less than three inches away, and got some really good pictures.

A ranger saw me doing this and screamed at me to be perfectly still. She was very alarmed and repeated that I should not move. The insects, she explained, were Tarantula Wasps, and they are cranky insects with nasty stings.

If I had stopped at the visitor's center first, the Rangers would have told me about any dangers in the local area. Although I got away without any issues, if I had been hiking or they hadn't warned me, I could have received a nasty sting.

Make it a habit to stop at the visitor center or ranger station when you arrive at your destination. Have a conversation with the rangers or other officials. They will be more than happy to tell you about the local conditions, weather, dangers, animals, and plants.

Explain to them where you plan to visit, how long you expect to be there, and what you are planning to do. During one visit to Joshua Tree National Park, the rangers told me about a spectacular bed of wildflowers a short distance from where I planned to be hiking. They thought I could get some excellent photographs of the spectacular flowers.

During a trip to Arches National Park, the rangers mentioned that I should photograph early in the morning because the sun would be shining directly through some of the arches. They thought these would be great photo opportunities.

The Rangers or officials are a fountain of knowledge about their park or scenic area. Take full advantage of their knowledge, both to learn about potential dangers and to find out how to better enjoy your visit.

Check the weather forecast

My friend and I decided to travel to San Jacinto State Park would be a great idea. It was early spring and the day was perfect; not too hot and not too cold. We each had a light jacket and expected a slightly nippy day.

We reached the base of the mountain and entered the tram. It was early, so there were only a couple of other travelers. The tram took us up to the top of the mountain, and we had lunch in the restaurant. Afterward, we went for a hike on a steep path down the back of the mountain. There was quite a bit of snow and ice from earlier storms, but the temperature was still warm.

After we had walked a good two miles, the sky became overcast, and the temperature dropped. We decided to hike back up the path, but at about the halfway point we were struck by a full-fledged blizzard. Fortunately, a couple of hikers had some blankets to spare and helped us get to the top of the mountain. However, we were cold, wet, and tired when we finally entered the restaurant.

It is a fact that the weather can change very fast. In the morning, it can be bright and sunny, only to change to overcast and cold by the afternoon. Rainstorms, even those 50 miles from your location, can cause flash floods. In the desert, a cool morning can change to a scorching afternoon, and along the beach an offshore storm in the ocean can cause swells and waves much larger than normal.

Subscribe to a weather service. If you log into the website of this kind of service and set your location accordingly, they can text you information such as flash flood and storm warnings.

Make sure you let people know

A friend of mine went on a trip to Yosemite National Park. She left on the spur of the moment, calling in sick to work, and drove to the park. She was intent on relaxing after a long month of hard work. Because she was playing hooky, she didn't tell anyone where she was going and hiked deep into the forest. She was miles from anyone when she fell and twisted her ankle. She spent a couple days lost in the forest before another hiker stumbled on her, literally, and got her some help.

It is essential to let someone know where you are going and when you will be returning. Give them your cell phone number, and if you can, the phone number of the ranger or visitor center, if there is one. When I travel I give a good friend my itinerary, plus the date and time I expect to return.

Make it a point to stop at the ranger station or visitor center and chat with them about your plans. Tell them where you expect to be within the area, and what times you plan to be there, which serves two purposes:

1. If someone needs to inquire about your whereabouts, the Rangers or workers in the office will have some idea where you are .
2. If there is some danger, such as a flash flood or fire, they can send out someone to find you.

Ensure you have the correct supplies

When I was young, my parents took the whole family on a long drive through the desert. There was no planning involved; they just decided one weekend we were going on a driving trip, so we got in the car and left.

The trip was a comical disaster. We ran out of gas, didn't have enough food, didn't bring any water, and did not prepare with the correct clothing for the cold desert nights.

When you are hiking or traveling, make sure you carry the appropriate supplies. For a driving trip, ensure you have food and water, at least, in your car. You should also carry emergency supplies (a first aid kit, fire extinguisher, flares and so on) and pack appropriate clothing. Always carry suntan lotion, and keep a few hats in the trunk to keep the sun off your head.

When I travel, I always carry a gallon or two of water in the trunk, along with some long-lasting food. I store two boxes of granola bars, one with nuts and one without, along with a bottle of peanuts, which gives me some carbohydrates and protein.

I also keep a watertight bag with toiletries in a suitcase in the car. The bag contains, for each person, a toothbrush, toothpaste, deodorant, and so on. This way they are available for long trips and emergencies. If my area is evacuated, my car already contains emergency supplies.

Include appropriate clothes for the weather. In fact, it's often a good idea to pack an extra set of clothing for longer day trips, just in case you find you have to stay overnight.

When you are hiking, be sure to include appropriate supplies. Bring sufficient water, food, and any medicines you require. Because you will be walking or hiking, bring more food than you think you will need.

Layer your clothing. As the temperature changes, you can remove or add layers as needed. And be sure to wear good hiking or walking shoes to protect your feet.

The idea is to be prepared and ready for contingencies. If you do this, you can relax and enjoy your trip, walk, hike, or whatever activity you are doing without concern.

Don't depend upon your GPS

In 2006, I decided to visit the Texas Renaissance Festival. I didn't check the weather before I left. When I arrived, the festival was open but it was pouring rain. Nevertheless, because I had flown all the way from California, I stayed and enjoyed the soggy festivities. After the festival had closed, I got in my car and began the 30-mile trip to my hotel.

I programmed the GPS unit that came with the rental car and proceeded on my way. It was a dark night because the sky was overcast, and there were no streetlights along the road. Before long I began to feel like I was driving down the road in the Texas Chainsaw Massacre. The road was narrow, it was pouring rain, and I had no idea where I was or how to get where I was going.

But I had my trusty GPS, so I was not worried; it would find the best route so I would arrive at my hotel safely. These things never fail, right?

Lightning flashed close by, way too close for comfort. A few minutes later my GPS told me to turn left. Obeying would have put my car in the middle of a lake. A minute later it informed me I was off the road, then on a freeway, then off the road again.

I could feel the panic rising. I was tired, hungry, and the place did remind me of a dark road in a horror movie. I kept driving, my hands tight on the steering wheel until I saw a light in the distance. I drove towards that illumination and soon was parked in front of a gas station.

A GPS is one thing most people who travel a lot depend on day in and day out. These small machines just work and keep working no matter what. They are very reliable and do an excellent job of getting you to where you are going.

On the other hand, the GPS tends to obscure our navigation abilities. In the past, before the GPS existed, if you wanted to get somewhere you pulled out a map and charted your course manually. I remember when it was quite common to stop at the AAA® office and get what was called a TripTik®, that was a manually created detailed booklets of maps getting you from one place to another.

After my adventure in Texas, I got in the habit of printing out a map using an online mapping application before leaving for my trip. These have come in handy, not just for the couple of occasions where the GPS failed, but also to get information about the surrounding areas

What to do when disaster strikes

Shelly and her family were watching the news when their television show was interrupted by an emergency broadcast bulletin. The dispassionate voice calmly announced that a Category 4 hurricane was predicted make landfall soon. Shelly knew her house was outside of the evacuation zone, so she could remain home even though her house was directly in the path of the storm.

Some disasters can be predicted. The National Weather Service is very good, although not perfect, at determining the strength and direction of a hurricane. Often towns and cities are evacuated a day or more in advance of the approaching storm.

Maps of evacuation zones are pre-published and are available on the local website for the city or county. It is important to obtain the maps in advance, as you may not have the time or ability to obtain them after an evacuation has been declared.

One evening in late November, Dave and his wife Sarah we startled awake by a major earthquake. They ran to the table located in the dining room, got underneath, and held onto the table legs. After the earth stopped shaking, they quickly inspected their home. Other than a few fallen bookshelves and some broken knick-knacks, everything was intact. They remained in their home for the next few days without power until the National Guard showed up.

Other disasters strike without warning. Fires, earthquakes, explosions, and industrial accidents don't come alert anyone before happening. In this kind of disaster, you have to ride it out the best you can and recover from the effects afterward.

Take pictures

Include a small camera in your go-bag, one that uses non-rechargeable batteries (if possible), with a few spare batteries. Use this to record damage and injuries, and even keep a journal of the events leading up to and after the disaster.

Photos will be useful in settling insurance claims and proving injuries to employers and others. If you have Internet connectivity, you can send photos via email to show friends and family that you and others are okay.

Also, snapping a few pictures now and then can calm the nerves, and you can make a very interesting photo album from them.

Earthquakes

When I lived in California, I did an inspection of my home with an eye toward earthquake preparation. As I looked around, I realized that my tables and desks all had glass tops. In fact, everything was covered in glass. If an earthquake occurred, there would have been nowhere for me to take cover. I replaced some of the glass-topped furniture with heavier, wooden models because I wanted to be able to get under something if the earth started moving.

Do you know what to do if the earth starts to shake? The choices you make within a couple of seconds after you feel the rippling of the ground may mean the difference between survival and death.

The biggest danger in an earthquake is falling debris. You need to get to cover to protect yourself from heavy objects.

Indoors
If you are indoors, here is what you should do:

1. Get on the floor.
2. Cover yourself under the most substantial furniture you can find fast. A heavy wooden desk or wooden table is perfect. Don't get under glass furniture.
3. If there is nothing to get under, crouch next to an interior wall.
4. Cover your head and neck with your arms and hold on to the furniture.
5. Move with the furniture (if you are under it) as it moves.

6. Stay there until the shaking stops.

Take cover away from anything that can topple over, such as a refrigerator or bookcase. Do not go running to help anyone else. Wait until the shaking stops.

Outdoors

In the outdoors, if you are near a building, get under a doorway. If you can, stay away from any electrical wires, power poles, and trees.

In large buildings, such as skyscrapers or apartment complexes, get under something and stay there until the earth stops shaking. Stay away from the elevators because these can fall or stick between floors.

You might be tempted to get under or beside a car. Resist that temptation. You'd be amazed at how much a car can bounce around in even a relatively mild earthquake.

While driving

Sometimes earthquakes happen while you are driving. Pull over as soon as you can, but try to park clear of any overpasses or power lines.

Triangle of Life and other methods to avoid

"Methods like standing in a doorway, running outside, and 'triangle of life' method are considered dangerous and are not recommended" – Earthquake County Alliance
http://www.earthquakecountry.info/dropcoverholdon/

Do *not* use the so-called Triangle of Life method (which states there is a "void" of safety next to objects). There is no safe area next to furniture or other objects. Get under a substantial piece of furniture such as a desk or table to protect yourself from falling debris.

Fire

One day I was at work, and the fire alarm started blaring. As I got up from my chair, I noticed that not a single person even raised their heads to look around. As it turned out, the alarm company was conducting a test, but I found the lack of concern about a fire alarm odd.

Fires spread fast. The moment you are aware of a fire, either due to the smell, fire alarm or a smoke detector, immediately head for the nearest exit. Don't panic, but get yourself and anyone in the area to safety. Once you are safe, call 911 to get help.

Obviously there are instances where fires can be put out with relative safety. I've smothered a couple of kitchen grease fires before they were dangerous and put out three trash can fires with fire extinguishers. If the fire is small and you keep calm they can be stopped before becoming serious.

However, when the fire gets beyond that, you need to get out. Fires can move quickly. Flames can block exits and smoke can disable you quickly. Fires can also travel underneath you, above you, and behind the walls.

If you are inside a room with a closed door, make sure you carefully touch the door with the back of your hand. If the door is warm or hot, do not open it; find a different way out.

Smoke and heat rise; drop to the floor and crawl to avoid breathing in fumes.

Hurricanes

Unlike many disasters, usually there is some notice of hurricanes. The weather service does a great job tracking and predicting these massive storms, and they send out periodic warnings so people can be prepared. If you sign up for one or more of the services in the chapter on *Disaster Information,* you should receive alerts of any impending storms. Of course, alerts are also broadcast on television and the radio.

Secure your home by closing storm shutters and doing whatever other preparation is required. Secure anything outside your home or bring it inside for storage.

Other tasks you should do before the storm hits include:

- Turn off any propane tanks.
- Turn your refrigerator and freezer to their coldest setting unless you are instructed to turn off utilities.
- Follow any other instructions given to you by the authorities.

You may need to evacuate:

- If ordered by the authorities.
- If you live near the beach or on a flood plain.
- If you live in any kind of mobile home. Do not remain in a mobile home or vehicle during a hurricane.
- During any other situation where you feel in danger.

Use your safe room if you have one. A safe room is a concrete shelter built according to FEMA standards to resist hurricanes and tornadoes. Close all interior doors, and secure and brace any exterior ones. If the weather calms down it may be the eye of the storm, so don't go outside until you get the all-clear from the authorities. As in other types of disasters, you may want to get under a table or other steady piece of furniture, and stay away from any objects that can fall over or fly around the room.

Flooding and storms

A friend of mine was taking his four-wheel drive vehicle for a spin in the desert. He was having a great time on the off-road trails when it started to rain. Since he was not walking, he felt safe and continued his fun. He drove in a streambed, just in time to get hit with the wall of water from a flash flood. He came home with a harrowing tale of almost drowning, the destruction of his car, and a rescue by a couple of Rangers.

Floods often occur during storms, and flash floods can occur without warning just about anywhere. Note that flash floods can occur even if the weather is sunny, because it could be raining on higher ground.

If you get a flash flood warning, get to higher ground immediately. If you are outdoors and it is raining, make sure get out of any streambeds, regardless of whether or not there is currently water in them.

Storms and flooding can cause many different issues, including:

- Downed power lines – stay away from them.
- Fast moving water in streets and streams – do not cross if the water is higher than your knees.
- Landslides – stay away from areas where landslides may or already have happened.
- Do not drive through flooded roadways or streams.
- If you are advised to evacuate, grab your go-bag and leave immediately.
- If your home is flooded, turn off the electricity at the circuit breakers.
- Use caution when entering flooded buildings, and wear shoes.
- Flood water, or anything that has been touched by it, should be considered contaminated. Do not drink water from any flooded location without purification.

Power outages

It was a very hot day in August. I was working at my computer in my home office when suddenly the lights and air conditioning switched off. We were without power for three days. The heat was more than 100 degrees, we had no way to cooking food, and even the alarm clocks didn't function. Driving to work was a nightmare because all of the traffic lights within a several miles radius were not working. Fortunately, the other utilities, including water, sewer, and phone service remained operational. We teamed up with the neighbors to barbecue food. I think the most dramatic effect was the reaction of our teenager to being without television and video games for such a long period; we thought he was going to go out of his mind.

The power grid is a complex web of wires, substations, power generators, and computers designed to deliver electricity to millions of homes and business at all hours of the day. To some extent, it can recover from damage by rerouting power through other lines.

Occasionally, though, power can fail over a widespread area. A significant emergency, such as fire, hurricane, earthquake, or tornado can cause this to happen. Also, the equipment required to generate and deliver power can fail, transmission lines can be damaged, and towers can collapse. All of these incidents can result in significant outages lasting hours, days, or longer.

Look around after a power outage to determine if it is local to just your home or is more widespread. If it's just your home or a few houses new you, report it to the electric company. It the outage appears to be large scale, they probably already know the power is out.

It's a good idea to turn off electronics when the power fails, which includes computers and any devices attached to them, as well as lights, the television, and so forth. Keep at least one light turned on. When the light turns on you will know when the power is back on.

If you use candles or other flammables for light and cooking, be careful of both the hazards from open flames as well as carbon monoxide poisoning. Ensure any candles or other flammables are safe from pets and children.

Do not use a generator inside your residence. The fumes given off can be deadly.

Finally, be careful when you drive or otherwise travel around town.

Food

Many of the disasters mentioned in this chapter will cause the power to fail. Your refrigerator and freezer will slowly heat up until the food inside is inedible.

You can safely eat the food in your refrigerator within four hours after the power fails. Keep the door closed as much as possible. Try not to open the door to the refrigerator more than necessary.

You can eat the food inside a typical freezer for 24 to 48 hours. A full refrigerator will remain cold longer than an empty one. A half-full freezer will keep food edible for 24 hours while a full will safely hold food for as long as 48 hours. Do not open the freezer door if you can avoid it.

Use a food thermometer to ensure any frozen or refrigerated food has not exceeded 40 degrees. Do not eat food that has warmed up beyond that point.

Eat the food from your refrigerator first, followed by frozen food, and finally the dry and canned goods you have stored in your home. The idea is to work your way from the most perishable foods to the least perishable.

Water

Water may be in short supply after a disaster. The municipal supply may be interrupted or contaminated.

As we discussed in the section on stocking up, it is best to store at least three days, and preferably two weeks, of water in your home. There are other places you can retrieve water to use after an emergency.

One important task after a disaster is to locate all sources of uncontaminated water in your home. You can take measures to ensure the water is not contaminated (for example, by shutting off the intake valve on the water heater), or you can drain it into containers for use later.

Decontaminating water

You may need to treat water before you can drink it because it may have been contaminated. You can use any of these methods:

- Use water purification tablets (recommended for your go-bag) to kill any bacteria.
- Add a small amount of chlorine bleach to the water. Make sure the bleach you use for this purpose contains only sodium hypochlorite

without soap or other chemicals. Check the label. In general, use 10 drops of store-bought household bleach per gallon of water purified. Let stand for 30 minutes. If you can still smell chlorine in the water, let it stand until the smell is gone.

- Boil the water.

Keep in mind that these methods only handle biological contamination. These methods will not be effective when the water has been polluted by chemicals.

Using the water in your water heater

Turn off the electrical power going to the water heater.

Normally, there is a valve at the bottom of the tank which is used to drain the water on occasion. There is probably a threaded pipe below this valve, and you can hook a garden hose up to that pipe. The valve may not have been opened for a while and could be fragile.

Before you attempt to drain the water from the tank, open any hot water tap in the building. The hot water in any kitchen or bathroom sink will do. Air needs to flow into the tank for the water to be drained.

The water may contain sediments (this is normal) so let it sit to allow these to sink to the bottom. Although there is little danger from drinking water drained from a water heater, to be safe, you can purify it by boiling, adding a small quantity of bleach, or using water purification tablets.

Toilets

You can use the water in the toilet tank providing it has not been contaminated by floodwaters or buried in debris. Water in the bowl must be considered unsafe to drink without being boiled or disinfected.

Ice Cubes

Don't forget about the ice cubes in your freezer. If the power goes out for any length of time get the ice cubes from your freezer and put them into a container. You can drink this later. If you leave it in the freezer, especially if the cubes are in a plastic bag, the water may drain away.

Cold

Emergencies such as blizzards, snowstorms, or just cold weather can create situations where you need to be concerned with how to keep yourself and your family warm. At first, this might not seem to be a huge problem. After all, everyone is cold once in a while. You just throw on a few blankets, maybe put some logs on the fire, and you're all set, right?

When your body temperature gets to 95 degrees Fahrenheit or below, you have a condition called hypothermia. This is a life-threatening situation, and you must act quickly to heat your body back up.

You can lose heat from any exposed portion of your skin. The most significant heat loss occurs from the head, neck, and wrists. If exposed to the cold, the arteries in your neck and wrists will transport that cold deep into the body and brain.

If you are outdoors, get to shelter as soon as possible. Protect yourself from the wind, and keep your breathing calm. Keep your body moving to keep the heat flowing and your blood pumping. Stay close to structures to block the window. Avoid walking through heavy snow drifts.

Layer your clothing, and if possible use something made of wool closest to your skin. Wool provides excellent insulation even when wet.

If your clothing gets wet, remove it as fast as possible. Wet clothes lose more than 90 percent of their insulating capabilities. Keep your clothes, shoes, and socks dry at all time. Remember that perspiration is moisture, so don't bundle up so much that you are perspiring heavily.

Except for fireplaces and candles, do not burn fires indoors. Fires give off smoke and carbon monoxide, which can lead to death.

Heat

A heat wave can be a disaster all by itself. Also, anything that knocks out the power can cause air conditioning to fail. In extreme heat, you can suffer from dehydration, which can lead to death.

Stay indoors in extreme heat. Keep your air conditioning on if the power hasn't failed. You can also go to the mall, library, or other building with air conditioning.

If you cannot use air conditioning, keep the windows on the shady side of the house open. Remember that as the sun moves overhead you may need to switch sides.

Shelter

Depending on the nature of the disaster, you may be forced to evacuate, or you might be able to ride it out at home.

Inspect your home as soon as you can after a disaster to determine if you can safely remain or if you need to find shelter somewhere else.

Evacuating

In 2005, the worst hurricane in United States history hit the Gulf coast like a sledgehammer hitting a piece of glass. Since the gulf coast gets slammed with major storms virtually every year, I would have thought they would have been prepared.

My sister-in-law was terrified and totally unprepared. She was forced to evacuate, was without any supplies, and her gas tank was close to empty. She left her home in a panic, waited in line at the gas station for half the day, then drove wildly across the state until she found a place to stay.

Meanwhile, we tried to keep track of her location from the west coast. Unfortunately, her cell phone stopped working (we later found the batteries ran out), and she didn't have any other way to contact us. For two weeks she and her family were missing until she finally found a place to send an email to us telling us she was okay.

Disasters happen at any time without warning. On occasion, you will need to evacuate the area. The authorities may order an evacuation or you may decide on your own that it is time to leave.

Sometimes, as with the approach of a hurricane, you'll get some warning and have time to pack up the car with supplies and whatever belongings you can carry. On the other hand, no one could have predicted the levees would break during Katrina, and earthquakes happen completely without notice.

A friend of mine, Sabrina, was teaching a class in her dance studio in San Diego. She was worried because the fires seemed very close, and the smoke was causing breathing issues among her students. It didn't surprise her when the police drove by and told them they needed to evacuate. The fires were getting too close for comfort.

Never assume your area is immune to evacuation. Evacuations can happen at any time and any place. A disaster can occur anywhere on the planet.

> Ned and his family were sleeping peacefully in their home in the middle of a small desert community. They were startled awake by a loud explosion; their bedroom was lit up by a huge fireball outside the window. They rushed outside to find that two trains had collided a few hundred yards from their home.
>
> One of the locomotives was hauling toxic chemicals, and these were leaking all over the ground and spewing into the air. After quickly conferring among themselves, Ned and his neighbors decided it was best to get in their cars and leave the area.

Evacuations are ordered to save lives. Authorities do not order large numbers of people to leave their homes and neighborhoods unless there is imminent danger of loss of life.

> There was a huge fire in Lake Arrowhead a few years ago. In fact, it was one of the largest fires in Southern California history. The fire threatened the small town, so an evacuation was ordered. The police and fire department got almost everyone out of the village, except for one man who refused to leave.
>
> The police were not happy with this situation. They knew the fire could change direction at any time, or the wind could pick up without warning, which meant there wouldn't be time or a way to get out. They forcibly removed the man, taking him to his car and telling him to drive away immediately.

Your disaster planning should include procedures for what to do if an evacuation is ordered. Discuss these procedures with your family and friends, those involved in your planning process, and ensure everyone understands their role.

Be sure to include your children in these discussions, which will help them mentally and emotionally if an evacuation occurs. Also, just the knowledge that plans exist, even if they don't fully understand them, can have a calming effect.

The hurricane had turned into a Category 4 storm and was headed directly towards Miami. The governor announced and evacuation on all of the local television and radio stations.

Sally and her family were ready because they had included evacuation procedures in their disaster planning. They grabbed their go-bags and put them into the trunk of their car, along with a case of water bottles, two cases of food, their medicines, and a couple of suitcases full of clothes. The trunk was packed, but they were well supplied.

Their gas tank was almost full, so they were able to drive 40 miles inland to the school gymnasium that was hurriedly converted into an evacuation center. The children were well behaved the entire time, and even helped pack the car, because they had been part of the disaster discussions and knew what to do.

In some areas, such as those potentially in the path of a hurricane, evacuation routes and procedures are determined in advance. For example, in Florida major storms are a possibility each year, so signs mark evacuation routes, and evacuee centers have been assigned beforehand.

You can find this information by checking with your local chamber of commerce. Also, many localities have set up websites that include all of the disaster information you'll ever need. The city or county website will include links to the information. You can also do a quick search using your favorite search engine to locate the data.

During the evacuation, be calm, follow the instructions given by authorities, and follow your plan the best that you can. Remember, though, that no plan survives a disaster. Having a plan makes it easier for you, but don't expect it to be perfect. Disasters tend to throw everything and everyone out of whack.

The gas station you expected to use might be without power. Your teenager could have forgotten to fill the gas tank the night before. The road could be blocked by a fallen tree, a bridge could be washed out, or a landslide could have destroyed everything.

Maintain the idea of flexibility as you plan for evacuation. You don't, and probably can't, plan for every contingency. You can prepare for evacuation by keeping supplies in the proper places (in a closet in your home and in the trunk of your car, for example), understanding evacuation routes, and having a good communication plan.

Wrapping it all up

Sometimes you can avoid creating a disaster by preparing properly for a trip or hike. Other disasters occur with little or no warning. Hurricanes, for example, can be predicted, but sometimes they change course or grow in intensity beyond what was expected.

Even though a disaster can strike anytime without warning, you can be prepared. You can maintain a good supply of water, food, and other supplies, and get some training from your local CERT group.

Your road to disaster preparedness begins with knowledge. Virtually everyone has the Internet at their fingertips these days, and you can use tools such as search engines and mapping software to learn more about the area in which you live.

Before going on a trip or excursion, spend a few minutes to check the weather, print out a map, and research your destination. A little knowledge can prevent major heartache or disappointment while you are on your trip.

I'll leave you with a final thought, and this is vital. You need to keep educating yourself, learning new things about survival. This is a never-ending process. You can't just read a book and put it back on the shelf.

Keep this book with you and keep it handy. Read it again every six to twelve months. You'll learn some new things with each reading. Supplement your knowledge by researching on the web, at your local library, and visiting your local fire department. Take and re-take the CERT class in your area occasionally; this gives you the opportunity to update your knowledge, ask questions, and learn any new information and skills.

Glossary

Category

Defines the speed of the winds in a hurricane.

- Category 1 winds of 74 to 95 mph
- Category 2 winds of 96 to 110 mph
- Category 3 winds of 111 to 130 mph
- Category 4 winds of 131 to 155 mph
- Category 5 winds greater than 156 mph

CERT

Community Emergency Response Team. A group organized by local fire departments to train civilians to be able to intelligently respond to an emergency situation.

Electrical panel

A box built into a wall, usually in a bedroom or closet, containing electrical circuits, switches, and surge protectors. Power in a home can be controlled from these panels.

FEMA

Federal Emergency Management Agency. The government agency which handles emergency preparation and responses.

Gas meter

A meter attached to most homes which measures and control the gas going into the house.

Go-bag

A bag filled with supplies and tools useful during a disaster. It is called a go-bag because you "grab the bag and go". Spend the time to properly equip a go-bag and you will have a much better chance of surviving a disaster.

GPS

Global Positioning System. In this context, refers to devices which aid in navigation. Generally, these allow the entry of locations, calculate the route to them, and display maps along the way.

Hurricane

A very violent storm, circular in nature, with winds greater than 74 mph.

Iodine capsules

Literally, capsules containing iodine. These are consumed after a nuclear disaster to help with the body's ability to resist radiation.

Levee

Also called a Dike. These are walls on the sides of a river or around an area to keep the water from intruding. Large portions of New Orleans are actually below sea level, and levees keep the water from the ocean from flooding into the city.

MRE

Meals Ready to Eat. Rations designed by the US military to provide for one third of a person's daily food requirement and store safely for the long term.

Situational Awareness

The concept of being aware of your surroundings.

Uninterruptable Power Supply

A large battery which acts as a surge protector and has enough power to keep a computer and some devices running for a few minutes in the event of a power failure.

Index

Recommended Reading

SAS Survival Handbook, Third Edition: The Ultimate Guide to Surviving Anywhere

by John 'Lofty' Wiseman

A complete guide on how to survive in any situation. The book decribes everything from how to be prepared all the way to surviving during a disaster and self-defense.

OUTDOOR LIFE - The Ultimate Survival Manual - 333 SKILLS That Will Get YOU Out Alive

by Simon & Schuster

This well illustrated, well written encyclopedia contains detailed information on every possible skill you might need during a disaster.

The Survival Medicine Handbook: A Guide for When Help is Not on the Way

by Joseph Alton and Amy Alton

When disaster strikes help may not be coming for days, weeks, or even months. It gives you the tools and insights to handle medical issues on your own.

About The Author

https://www.linkedin.com/in/richardlowejr

Richard Lowe has leveraged more than 35 years of experience as a senior computer manager and designer at four companies into that of an author, blogger, ghost writer, and public speaker. He has written hundreds of articles for blogs and ghost written more than a dozen books. He's published factual books about computers, the Internet, surviving disasters, management, and human rights. He's currently working on a ten-volume science fiction series, to be published at the rate of three volumes per year beginning in 2016.

After living through the experience of an earthquake, Richard decided to take a CERT (Community Emergency Response Team) class. He enjoyed the class so much he took it twice, then read everything he could find about surviving a disaster. Richard decided to write this book to pass on to people some tips to enable them to prepare for and get through disasters of all kinds.

Richard began in the field of Information Technology, first as the Vice President of Consulting at Software Techniques, Inc. Because he craved action, after six years he moved on to work at two companies at the same time: - he was a Vice President at Beck Computer Systems and the Senior Designer at BIF Accutel. In January 1994, he found a home at Trader Joe's as the Director of Technical Services and Computer Operations. He remained at that wondrous company for almost 20 years, before taking an early retirement to begin a new life as a professional writer. He is currently the CEO of The Writing King, a company which provides all forms of writing services, and the Senior Writer, Business Division, for The Ghost Publishing.

Richard has a quirky sense of humor and has found that life is full of joy and wonder. As he puts it, "this little ball of rock, mud, and water known as Earth is an incredible place, with many secrets to discover. Our corner of the universe is filled with beings, some happy and some sad, who each have their own special story to tell."

His philosophy is to take life with a light heart; He approaches each day as a new source of happiness. Evil is ignored, discarded or defeated; Good gets helped, enriched and fulfilled.

Richard spent many happy days hiking in many national parks, crawling over boulders, and peering at Indian pictographs. He toured the Channel Islands off Santa Barbara, and stared in fascination at wasps building their homes in

Anza-Borrego. Some of his joys include photography, and he has photographed more than 1,200 belly dance events as well as dozens of renaissance fairs all over the country.

Because writing is his passion, Richard remains extremely creative and prolific; each day he completes between 5,000 and 10,000 words, diligently using language to bring the world to life so that others may learn and be entertained.

You can find out more at http://www.thewritingking.com and emails are welcome at rich@thewritingking.com

Colophon

All text written by Richard G. Lowe Jr.

This book was written using Microsoft Word 2013. Graphics were editing using Paint Shop Pro X7. The font used throughout the manuscript is Georgia.

The front cover was designed and created by Crownzgraphics. Their email address is crownzgraphics@gmail.com. The back cover was created by Richard G. Lowe Jr using Paint Shop Pro X7.

Joe Wisinski edited and proofread the manuscript.

The manuscript was reviewed by Susan Jekarl at
https://www.linkedin.com/pub/susan-jekarl/9/8bb/a50
Check out her site at: www.totallyunprepared.com

You can find up-to-date information at the Real World Survival blog at
http://www.realworldsurvival.com

This book is published by The Writing King. Paperback version is published via Createspace. Kindle version is published via Kindle Direct Publishing.

The Writing King website: http://www.thewritingking.com

Other web sites operated by Richard Lowe Jr:
Personal website: http://www.richardlowe.com
Photography: http://www.richardlowejr.com
LinkedIn Profile: https://www.linkedin.com/in/richardlowejr

If you have any comments about this book, feel free to email Richard G. Lowe Jr at rich@thewritingking.com

Notes

Notes

Notes

Notes

Notes

Made in the USA
Lexington, KY
29 August 2015